T0271437

Ethical Consumption

Arising from foundations in green and eco-consumerism, ethical consumption is a multidisciplinary area of research. This shortform book presents an expert view of the empirical evidence on ethical consumption, incorporating perspectives from marketing, psychology and sociology.

It takes both a historical and a thematic perspective, covering definitions of ethical consumption, typologies of ethical consumer practices, successes brought about from consumer actions and the current challenges. It also focuses on the emergence of contemporary perspectives on ethical consumer behaviour from three discrete perspectives: those focusing on consumer segmentation (the profiling of ethical consumers), those which take a psychological approach (the decision-making processes which underpin ethical consumption) and those which are sociological in nature (the identities and practices which underpin ethical consumption). The book finally synthesises these perspectives in the context of the 'problems' that are often claimed to exist, such as the existence of the 'attitude–behaviour gap', and provides conclusions which make recommendations for practice and further research.

It will be of interest to academics and students of marketing, consumption and related fields, as well as to practitioners and policymakers who want to understand more about the evidence pertaining to ethical consumers, what motivates them, and how to encourage and educate them to consume more ethically.

Alex Hiller is Head of Postgraduate and Executive Education at Nottingham Business School, Nottingham Trent University, UK.

Helen Goworek is Associate Professor in Marketing at Durham University Business School, Durham University, UK.

State of the Art in Business Research
Series Editor: Geoffrey Wood

Recent advances in theory, methods and applied knowledge (alongside structural changes in the global economic ecosystem) have presented researchers with challenges in seeking to stay abreast of their fields and navigate new scholarly terrains.

State of the Art in Business Research presents shortform books which provide an expert map to guide readers through new and rapidly evolving areas of research. Each title will provide an overview of the area, a guide to the key literature and theories and time-saving summaries of how theory interacts with practice.

As a collection, these books provide a library of theoretical and conceptual insights, and exposure to novel research tools and applied knowledge, that aid and facilitate in defining the state of the art, as a foundation stone for a new generation of research.

Emergency Services Management
A Research Overview
Paresh Wankhade and Peter Murphy

Cultural Management
A Research Overview
Chris Bilton

Ethical Consumption
A Research Overview
Alex Hiller and Helen Goworek

For more information about this series, please visit: www.routledge.com/State-of-the-Art-in-Business-Research/book-series/START

Ethical Consumption
A Research Overview

Alex Hiller and Helen Goworek

Routledge
Taylor & Francis Group

LONDON AND NEW YORK

First published 2023
by Routledge
4 Park Square, Milton Park, Abingdon, Oxon OX14 4RN

and by Routledge
605 Third Avenue, New York, NY 10158

Routledge is an imprint of the Taylor & Francis Group, an informa business

© 2023 Alex Hiller and Helen Goworek

British Library Cataloguing-in-Publication Data
A catalogue record for this book is available from the British Library

Library of Congress Cataloging-in-Publication Data
Names: Hiller, Alex, 1977– author. | Goworek, Helen, author.
Title: Ethical consumption: a research overview / Alex Hiller and Helen Goworek.
Description: Abingdon, Oxon; New York, NY: Routledge, 2023. |
Series: State of the art in business research |
Includes bibliographical references and index.
Identifiers: LCCN 2022060826 (print) | LCCN 2022060827 (ebook) |
ISBN 9781032160634 (hardback) | ISBN 9781032160641 (paperback) |
ISBN 9781003246954 (ebook)
Subjects: LCSH: Consumption (Economics)–Moral and ethical aspects. |
Consumer behavior–Moral and ethical aspects.
Classification: LCC HB835 . H55 2023 (print) |
LCC HB835 (ebook) | DDC 178–dc23/eng/20230118
LC record available at https://lccn.loc.gov/2022060826
LC ebook record available at https://lccn.loc.gov/2022060827

ISBN: 978-1-032-16063-4 (hbk)
ISBN: 978-1-032-16064-1 (pbk)
ISBN: 978-1-003-24695-4 (ebk)

DOI: 10.4324/9781003246954

Typeset in Times New Roman
by Newgen Publishing UK

Contents

Acknowledgements   vi

1 Introduction   1

2 Ethical consumption: Definitions and development   4

3 Segmentation perspectives on ethical consumption   16

4 Psychological perspectives on ethical consumption   26

5 Sociological perspectives on ethical consumption   37

6 Problems in ethical consumption research   47

7 Conclusion: Observations on state of the art   59

   References   63
   Index   80

Acknowledgements

Our thanks go to all our colleagues and collaborators who have supported and informed our thinking in producing this book. In particular thanks to Dr Tony Woodall and Prof Mollie Painter at Nottingham Business School, Nottingham Trent University, for their advice and insight. We would also like to thank the reviewers of earlier drafts for their helpful and constructive comments.

1 Introduction

This book focuses on ethical consumption in which interest has grown significantly, both in its volume and in terms of the range of concerns which underpin it, with far-reaching effects on business and society. The social consciousness of customers has long been recognised; indeed, Newholm et al. (2015) argue that ethical consumption is a recurrent, not new, market phenomenon, with examples of ethics in individual consumption being evident from the late eighteenth century onwards, such as the 1791 UK consumer boycott against slave-produced sugar. However, whilst modern business ethics can be traced back to the USA in the early 1970s (Mahoney, 1994) with studies of socially concerned consumers also appearing at this time, interest in the ethicality of a number of products and services and associated consumer behaviour has been increasing in recent years.

Gabriel and Lang (2006) note that consumer organisations focused on green and ethical concerns, such as the FairTrade Foundation, accelerated in the 1980s after a slow start in the 1970s, although these organisations did not achieve any real coherence until the last few years of the twentieth century. Similarly, a wave of consumer activism in the 'green 90s' has galvanised into a progressive consumer 'political activism' which includes ethical, social and ecological dimensions and which has increasingly affected the high street and 'mainstream' consumers. Company responses have followed a corresponding trajectory, although these have not been without their problems. For example, in the early 1990s, some major UK retailers experimented with the introduction of so-called eco women's clothing ranges, but they do not appear to have been commercially successful, perhaps because they were either ahead of their time or the ranges were not promoted sufficiently. However, as Davies and Gutsche (2016) note, 'green' and 'eco' ranges, Fair Trade and organic products, and company transparency over environmental

DOI: 10.4324/9781003246954-1

performance and supply chain issues are increasingly key features of the 'mainstream' business landscape.

Correspondingly, studies of the role of ethics in consumer purchasing behaviour have gathered pace, moving from a relatively niche concern in the latter years of the twentieth century, to becoming a prominent feature of academic research from the mid-2000s onwards. Whilst, as Carrington et al. (2021) observe, ethical consumption been explored not only in the fields of business, management and economics, but also in perspectives from the arts and humanities, psychology and social sciences, the business, marketing and consumer behaviour literature has seen a particular growth in studies exploring this increasingly prominent dimension of consumption, especially in (but not limited to) Western societies.

Against this background, in this book we will present an overview of the development of this research on ethical consumption, taking both a historical and a thematic perspective on the field as follows: in Chapter 2, we offer the identification and definitions of ethical consumption and related terminology and note relevant distinctions between this terminology. We explore typologies of ethical consumer practices (and 'ideal' models of consumer behaviour) and offer a brief discussion of consumer power and the extent to which consumers can be considered to be morally culpable for their purchases. From this we aim to identify both successes brought about from consumer action and provide an overview of current challenges and criticisms in the field. We then focus on the emergence of contemporary perspectives on ethical consumer behaviour from three discrete perspectives which we believe are salient in the business and marketing literature on ethical consumption. We argue these approaches not only broadly follow the broad historical trajectory of research in the field but also characterise three dominant schools of thought in the business and marketing literature. Firstly, we explore what we have termed segmentation perspectives, or research focusing on the profiling and characteristics of ethical consumers. Secondly, we explore perspectives which take a psychological/cognitive approach, or research which seeks to understand the decision-making processes which underpin ethical consumption. Thirdly, we identify perspectives which are broadly sociological in nature. That is, those which focus on the identities and practices which underpin ethical consumption. These latter perspectives are key, as the dominant perspective in much of the 'early' ethical consumption literature implied the consumer as 'rational maximiser' (Newholm et al., 2015), making largely conscious and utilitarian decisions, whereas other studies have recognised the critical importance of the cultural context of consumption, including customer identity. We will then synthesise these perspectives in the context of the 'problems' that are often claimed to exist in ethical consumption, not least in the existence of the 'attitude–behaviour gap' and provide conclusions which make recommendations for practice and further research.

2 Ethical consumption
Definitions and development

Defining ethical consumption and its scope

A number of related terms have been used to characterise the growing ethical consumer movement such as green consumerism (de Groot et al., 2016), eco-consumerism (Dauvergne and Lister, 2010), conscious consumerism (Godwin, 2009), sustainable consumption (Pinto et al., 2014) and socially responsible consumerism (Han and Stoel, 2017). However, we take a broad approach in line with the scope of ethical consumption having widened from 'green' (which has become less popular in its usage due to its amorphous nature and its use in negative business practices such as 'greenwashing') or 'eco' consumer activism to include those positive choice consumption behaviours which benefit society and the environment. These may also include the avoidance or boycott of companies considered not to hold normative ethical standards (Szmigin et al., 2009) as a response to the increasing recognition of ethical, social and ecological impacts of production and consumption. The United Nations have reflected this in their Sustainability Development Goals, and in particular Goal 12 'Sustainable Production and Consumption' which, as cited within the Johannesburg Plan of Implementation, involves a range of stakeholders to: "accelerate the shift towards sustainable consumption and production to promote social and economic development … through improving efficiency and sustainability in the use of resources and production processes and reducing resource degradation, pollution and waste" (p.7). We contend that the term 'ethical consumption' should be distinguished from that of 'consumer ethics', the latter of which typically relates to the unethical practices of consumers such as stealing, illegal downloading/copying, dishonesty or otherwise seeking to gain some form of unfair advantage (see, for example, Vitell and Muncy, 2005).

DOI: 10.4324/9781003246954-2

Table 2.1 The range of ethical issues

Ethical issues	Example studies
Sweatshop avoidance	Shaw et al., 2007
Fair Trade	Ma et al., 2012; Kim et al., 2010; Connolly and Shaw, 2006; Shaw et al., 2006; Littrell et al., 2005; Low and Davenport, 2005
Company ethical codes of conduct	Iwanow et al., 2005
Labour abuses in the supply chain	Hyllegard et al., 2009; Moor and Littler, 2008; Valor, 2007
Organic products	Lim et al., 2014; Hustvedt and Dickson, 2009

The range of ethical issues which could be covered by such ethical, ecological and social impacts are shown in Table 2.1.

Connolly and Shaw (2006) argue that despite this apparent diversity in consumer concerns, there are common identifiable characteristics, and they therefore propose three broad headings under which these can be grouped: green consumerism, ethical consumerism and voluntary simplicity. A wider body of ethical concerns is represented by Memery et al. (2005) who cite three ethics and social responsibility clusters (in relation to the grocery market): quality and safety, human rights and ethical trading, and environmental (green) issues. A wider application again is given by *Ethical Consumer* magazine's product ratings across five dimensions:

• Environment (which includes environmental reporting, nuclear power, climate change, pollution and toxins, and habitats and resources);
• Animals (which includes animal testing, factory farming and animal rights);
• People (which includes human rights, workers' rights, supply chain policy, irresponsible marketing, and arms and military supply);
• Politics (which includes political activity, boycott calls, genetic engineering, antisocial finance and company ethos);
• Product sustainability (which includes the presence of certification schemes such as organic, Fair Trade, the TCO environmental label, EU energy label, certification from the Vegan or Vegetarian Societies, or other sustainability features not covered by certification schemes).

We would recommend caution, however, in viewing these issues as discrete entities. As Connolly and Shaw (2006) observe, the distinction between 'green' and 'ethical' is ambiguous due to the interconnectivity between the various concerns; in particular environmental and Fair Trade concerns are often coupled together. They note, for example, that ethical consumers were often confused about which was 'best': food which had the least environmental impact (for example, organic vegetables) or which was fairly traded. Likewise, Newholm (2005) notes that specific consumer practices should not be seen in isolation and that the range of potential ethical concerns mentioned above will often overlap.

Ethical consumption practices

A number of authors have attempted to clarify the forms in which these consumer choices and responsibilities might manifest themselves, and what might therefore be included under the heading of 'ethical consumer behaviour'. For example, Harrison et al. (2005) propose a typology of five ethical consumer practices:

- Boycotts (refusing to buy certain products/brands)
- Positive buying (for example, buying 'Fair Trade')
- Fully screened (using consumer guides and ratings to make choices)
- Relationship purchasing (attempting to change the behaviour of suppliers)
- Anti-consumerism (avoiding unsustainable products such as cars or pursuing DIY alternatives such as mending rather than replacing clothes, often referred to as 'voluntary simplicity').

Newholm and Shaw (2007), in their review of the research around the ethics of consumption, identify six interlinked ways in which consumers may express themselves in such a way, and associated areas of study: consumer ethics relating to 'misbehaviour', consumer resistance to marketing efforts, individual and semi-organised projects related to sustainability (such as downshifting or voluntary simplicity), entrepreneurial efforts in relation to creating ethical consumption opportunities and spaces (perhaps often tied to political action), expert academic perspectives on the ethics of consumption and ethical consumption as a conscious project. Shaw and Riach (2011) distinguish between those forms of market resistance (such as boycotting, consumer rebellion, countercultural movements and non-consumption) and relational interactions *with* the market, and this relational approach enhances understanding of how consumers negotiate their market choices. Some researchers, as noted by Schmitt et al. (2022), have gone so far as to begin to reject the word *consumer*, which carries the implication of the destructive nature of consumption itself. However, it is important to recognise that all these categorisations imply both the consumption practices of ethically engaged or committed consumers, and the consumption of ethically produced products and services more generally. It should be recognised that ethically committed individuals may not necessarily be constantly engaged in ethical consumption, but likewise the consumption of ethically produced goods and services may be undertaken by any consumer, whether categorised as 'ethically committed' or not.

It should also be noted that the definitions above perhaps overlook a possible interaction (and mutual influence) between a reactive kind of ethical awareness amongst consumers which arises due to ethical *failures* and a proactive concern to influence ethical business practices via consumer choices. A key question therefore arises around whether ethical consumption is a 'knee-jerk' reaction against unethical business practices or something that emerges from consumers' personal goals – punishment versus reward, if you will. Furthermore, Miller (2012) identifies a third type of moral consumption in relation to the latter; one which is not 'other'-oriented as most definitions of ethical consumption explicitly or implicitly acknowledge but a morality which might be characterised by thrift and duty to the family. What emerges is that definitions of ethical consumption behaviours and the ethical concerns that underpin them are multidimensional, dynamic and often context-specific.

The impact of ethical consumption

Corporate social responsibility

These considerations and impacts have provoked significant and mainstream business and consumer responses. At the industry level, the response to these concerns has been through the adoption of the number of standards and product certification/labelling schemes that have arisen globally, and the rise of the B-Corp movement (companies verified by the B Lab organisation as having high social and environmental standards), social purpose corporations and low-profit limited liability companies (Stobierski, 2021). Indeed, the rise of standards has been meteoric; Hohnen and Potts (2007) identified over 250 initiatives and standards relevant to corporate social responsibility (CSR) in existence, and the *OECD* (2009) noted 'hundreds' of initiatives which offer guidance on social and environmental issues. Environmental, social and governance criteria have become standards sought by socially conscious investors when making investment decisions, as a further level of ethical consumption (de Spiegeleer et al., 2022).

As Stobierski (2021) notes, CSR is usually potentially categorised in four ways: environmental responsibility (behaving in an environmentally friendly way such as reducing pollution or regulating energy consumption), ethical responsibility (ensuring businesses operate in a fair and transparent manner), philanthropic responsibility (making the world and society a better place) and economic responsibility (not only maximising profits, but backing its financial decisions in service of its other responsibilities). This reflects the 'triple bottom line' of planet, people and profit (Elkington, 1999). Over the last 20 years, studies have provided evidence that the ethics or social responsibility of companies impact consumer decision-making through 'positive purchasing behaviour' (see, for example, Moraes, et al., 2017; Ha-Brookshire and Norum, 2011; Connolly and Shaw, 2006; Littrell et al., 2005). However, whilst a number of ethical codes and standards exist, these often focus on a variety of specific issues and it is unlikely that there is a 'best' standard which may account for the breadth of potential concerns. As Shaw and Riach (2011) note, the term 'ethics', as it applies to ethical consumption, has been interpreted from a number of different standpoints. This perhaps highlights a failure in research and practice to deal with the numerous and complex cognitive ('rational'), affective ('emotional') and conative ('behavioural') concerns that consumers may have. In addition, many of the standards have been criticised from various viewpoints, either for failing to enforce the practices they promote, for providing an insufficient 'level' of 'ethicality' or for 'displacing' ethical problems (for example, Fair Trade products causing over-supply, or organic products causing further deforestation). The question of how ethics should be approached is therefore critical in undertaking any analysis of ethical consumption. As Caruana (2007) argues, a clear definition of morality is absent from the consumption literature, and this is especially important where consumption is treated sociologically and not just as another cognitive factor impacting purchase decisions. This will be explored further in Chapters 4 and 5.

A challenge, therefore, in addressing codes of ethics is helping consumers to identify ethical issues which relate to their concerns. As previously discussed, the terminology surrounding various dimensions of ethics is often used interchangeably, and as Carrigan and De Pelsmacker (2009) note, consumer confusion is often cited as a key barrier to buying more sustainably. Furthermore, the concept of *sustainability* is perhaps most often applied by industry and governments, often defined broadly (and arguably most widely) in line with the Brundtland Commission's definition: "... the principle of ensuring that our actions today do not limit the range of economic, social and environmental options open to future generations" (Elkington, 1999, p.20). This is also in accordance with Elkington's (1999) 'triple bottom line', which focuses on economic prosperity, environmental quality and social justice. Economic capital comprises physical capital, financial capital, human capital and intellectual capital. Thus, organisations must consider not only their economic sustainability in terms of whether demand for products and services and profit margins are sustainable and whether costs are competitive, but also whether the rate of innovation is competitive and how to ensure that human and intellectual capital remain within the organisation. 'Social accounting' could cover community relations, product safety, education and training initiatives, charitable donations, employment of disadvantaged groups, poverty alleviation, upholding human rights and employment creation. The environmental 'bottom line' is discussed in terms of natural capital – both capital which is essential to the maintenance of life and ecosystem integrity, and capital which can be renewed, repaired, substituted or replaced. The final element, the social bottom line, is the one that Elkington (1999) claims businesses had, at that point, traditionally overlooked; this comprises human capital (public health, skills and education) and wider measures of a society's health and wealth-creation potential; the trust between organisations and stakeholders is key here in allowing social relationships to prosper.

The domain of business ethics is considered to lie in the zone between the social and economic bottom lines (and Elkington acknowledges the problems in assessing ethical behaviours). However, it is likely that the scope of business ethics is much wider than considered, under the social bottom line of sustainability but falling within the broader domain of CSR (Schwartz and Carroll, 2003). Fisher (2004) cites the work of Davidson and Griffin, who suggest that individuals 'have' ethics, whereas organisations 'have' a social responsibility; the ethical beliefs of consumers may then 'cut across' business ethics, CSR and sustainability. Thus, organisations can create value in multiple dimensions; in the case of sustainability, this value is referred to in terms of environmental, social and economic value added or destroyed. Indeed, there are parallels to draw between the triple bottom line and with Schwartz and Carroll's (2003) 'three domain model' of CSR, which includes economic responsibilities (defined by the economic bottom line), legal responsibilities and issues of environmental and social responsibilities classified under (but not exclusively contributing towards) 'ethical' responsibilities. It should be noted, however, that a potential problem with the triple bottom line approach is that economic efficiencies can often be given priority over social and environmental factors (Dianati and Banfield, 2020).

Ethical consumption at the organisational level

At the organisational level, concern over the ethics of various business practices and the growth in 'ethical markets' has led to the emergence of organisations, overtly positioned as 'ethical', which adopt a values-led purpose and which characterise 'positive purchasing'. It is argued that such values-led organisations appeal to customers on the basis of more than a product, as they offer consumers a way to express their own most deeply held values. However, as argued by Mish and Miller (2014), as consumers place more emphasis on environmental and social impacts, companies more clearly express these values and work actively on product development and production processes, reflect environmental and social costs in value propositions, reduce waste in distribution systems and increasingly promote sustainable business practices. Indeed, according to the Edelman Trust Barometer (2021), trust is 'the new brand equity', as highly trusted brands are seven times more likely to be purchased and consumers will give up brands that they love if they don't trust them. According to their research, business integrity (which includes addressing climate change, alleviating poverty, good corporate citizenship and playing a role in improving social issues) is the key to building trust, and therefore brands will need to operate at the intersection of culture, purpose and society. Similarly, the Zeno (2020) *Strength of Purpose* study finds that a significant, positive relationship exists between strength of organisational purpose and business results. Here, 'purpose' defines an organisation's role in society that allows it to grow and positively impact the world, and which has become more important to consumers and investors with social consciousness higher than ever. As Knowles et al. (2022) note, 'cause' (or social good-based) purpose creates maximum visibility for companies that push for societal change (although, of course, this must be genuine and embedded within company culture).

Ethical consumption is therefore a significant issue for organisations, since they have an opportunity to respond by meeting consumers' ethical requirements, thus addressing social and/or environmental sustainability whilst also contributing to their own financial sustainability by providing products and services which meet consumer demand. CSR policies can mirror consumers' ethical attitudes and practice, demonstrating to customers that organisations hold similar values to themselves, in an iterative process which can encourage companies and their customers to enhance their ethical behaviours. Indeed, as Brinkmann (2004) suggests, moral responsibilities should be seen as a shared responsibility between business and consumers. Previous research has acknowledged that ethical consumption can be influential within the business environment (for example, Sebastiani et al., 2013; Jayawardhena et al., 2016). Pivato et al. (2008) found that gaining consumer trust was a significant link between CSR and consumer actions in the organic food sector. Castaldo et al. (2009) established a further connection between CSR and consumer trust, conditional upon companies both committing to protect consumers' rights and offering products which comply with ethical requirements. Organisations that do not respond to ethical consumption requirements risk losing competitive advantage, since competitors may consequently match customers' ethical requirements more effectively. Similarly, Deng and Xu (2017) find that CSR has positive effects on consumer purchase intention and word of mouth. Consequently, CSR has come to be seen as a key strategic business issue (Kuokannen and Sun, 2020). However, companies need to take care not to over-promote their ethical credentials, since this can lead to accusations of greenwashing (Schmuck et al., 2018) from activists, the media, consumers and other stakeholders. For example, a business could promote a token environmentally sustainable feature of a product, whereas the majority of the materials used in its manufacture are unsustainable.

Ethical consumption at the sector level

Much of the research into ethical consumption has focused on a small number of discrete consumer sectors, in particular groceries (see, for example, Jayawardhena et al., 2016; Memery et al., 2005), clothing (see, for example, Hiller and Woodall, 2019; Ha-Brookshire and Norum, 2011), travel and tourism (see, for example, Malone et al., 2014) and luxury products (see, for example, Moraes et al., 2017). A number of others have sought to explore issues related to Fair Trade and organic products. Correspondingly, in the UK, the Cooperative (2021) Ethical Consumer Markets report notes that the most significant growth in low-carbon home and lifestyle spending has been in eco-travel and transport, green home (including energy), and ethical food and drink (72.6%, 34.6% and 12.3% growth, respectively, over a ten-year period). Ethical personal products (clothes and cosmetics), ethical finance and local shopping also saw strong growth, however. A UK market study by

Mintel (2022a) notes that there is increasing interest in sustainability, which 'represents an important window for growth', reporting that 53% of consumers would be more likely to prioritise sustainability in their purchase decisions for products for the home, than they would have done two years earlier. Mintel (2022b) also credits sustainable innovations for contributing to a reverse in the previously declining UK sportswear market. Mintel (2022c) have found that most young men aged under 35 in their sample were becoming increasingly environmentally conscious when shopping for clothing, thus driving fashion retailers to become more ethically responsible.

Ethical consumption at the individual (consumer) level

As the above suggests, ethical consumption has in recent years moved from being a 'niche' issue to a more mainstream consumer concern (Davies and Gustche, 2016). For example, Carrigan and De Pelsmacker (2009) note that in the four years from 2005 to 2009, the percentage of UK consumers reporting buying Fair Trade products rose from 20% to almost half. The latest Cooperative (2021) Ethical Consumer Markets report claims that ethical consumer spending and finance in the UK hit record levels at the end of 2020 with the overall market for ethical goods and services rising to £122bn from just £11.2bn in 1999. It notes that the emergence of the government's Net Zero Strategy is likely to drive transformative change in our lives and consumer spending. An Accenture (2020) survey of consumers across 15 countries further found that during the Covid-19 pandemic, consumer focus on ethical consumption had increased and that this is one of a number of changes in consumer behaviour that is likely to endure. The UK Cooperative (2021) Ethical Consumer Markets report reports that average spend per household on ethical products and services was £2189 per annum (a 113% growth since 2010). Despite the current global economic challenges, evidence from the previous (2008) global economic downturn (Carrigan and De Pelsmacker, 2009) suggests that ethical consumers continue to purchase in accordance with their values, even in the face of price premiums, provided direct benefits are offered. Further, 'mainstream' consumers had adopted what were traditionally considered to be ethical consumer practices (such as trading down and 'making do') in an attempt to save money. With a renewed focus on supply chain issues which have caused major brands such as Nike, Unilever and Adidas to retain commitments to ethical sourcing and manufacture, and with renewed commitments to the transition to net-zero, the challenge for organisations is to retain commitments to improving standards, raising consumer education and seeking efficiencies in supply chains without reducing commitments to ethical standards.

Increasingly, consumers are being recognised as 'citizen consumers' who exercise their power in the marketplace in the ways described above and which can be seen as expressions of consumer voting (Moraes et al., 2011). Schwartz (2010) further characterises the moral connection between consumers and products as 'the consumer as complicit participant'. As Inglehart and Welzel (2005) observe, the rise of self-expression values and the empowerment brought about by human emancipation have given rise not to the promotion of selfishness but to the maximisation of human well-being, forcing organisations to be responsive to people as they become increasingly empowered. It is for these reasons, perhaps, that issues such as Fair Trade and sustainability have become important to consumers. This perception of power may therefore be an important determinant of ethical consumption. It should be recognised, however, that there is a danger in the 'consumption as voting' paradigm. As Low and Davenport (2007) assert, the 'mainstreaming' of ethical purchasing from niche markets to the high street has resulted in a loss of focus from highly politicised programmes designed to affect social change to a more diminished form of individualised 'shopping for a better world' (p.336). That is, that there are limits to individual consumer decision-making in this 'de-politicised' space which are unlikely to result in social and/or political change.

Problems with ethical consumption

However, the effectiveness of both industry and consumer responses has been challenged. In terms of industry responses, as Painter-Morland (2011) notes, doubts about the effectiveness of codes and standards are often expressed by business ethicists, with common criticisms being that they reduce ethics to an issue of compliance, with little scope within them to reflect what is really valued by an organisation's stakeholders. For example, one of the most widely recognised ethical codes adopted by clothing retailers in the UK and Europe is the Ethical Trading Initiative (ETI) which has previously come under criticism for failing to sufficiently address freedom of association and discrimination (Barrientos and Smith, in Hughes et al., 2007) and for its failure to 'police' or accredit its members (Birch, 2007). Further, Hughes et al. (2007) note that the global management of ethical trade through such standards depends largely on the national–institutional context, and that industry governance is increasingly becoming controlled by an elite group of globalising retailers. Similarly, even widely known and adopted standards relating to manufacture and production such as Fair Trade and organic certification have come under fire. For example, *The Economist* (2006) argued that Fair Trade depresses prices rather than keep them high as it prevents farmers from diversifying into other crops, resulting in overproduction, and that a small percentage of the markup on Fair Trade goods actually goes to the farmer. Griffiths (2011) further argues that Fair Trade unequally benefits the richest farmers and further increases the poverty of those poorest farmers not Fair Trade certified, and as consumers are not informed of to whom in the supply chain the premiums are paid (and how much), the scheme promotes unfair trading. There remains, therefore, a question around whether the answer to these problems lies not in consumer choices but in political change. Businesses in the industry have also been criticised for being slow to act, even in response to major and very public disasters such as the *Rana Plaza* collapse (Clean Clothes Campaign, 2013; Neville, 2015).

The effectiveness of ethical consumption itself has also been questioned by many. Indeed, as recognised by Newholm et al. (2015), ethical consumption is highly complex and unpredictable. Critical perspectives on ethical consumption have acknowledged problems on grounds including consumer uncertainty and a lack of knowledge about ethical decision-making (Hassan et al., 2013; Hiller Connell, 2010), the existence of the 'attitude–behaviour gap' and its underlying 'causes' (Carrington et al., 2014; Johnstone and Tan, 2015; Moraes et al., 2012), neutralisation techniques (Chatzidakis et al., 2004) and the employment of rationalisation strategies including economic rationalisation, institutional dependency and developmental realism (Eckhardt et al., 2010). A host of other factors have been summarised by Littler (2011), including the role of ethical consumption in relieving middle-class guilt, its roles as a form of individual politics or in satisfying profit-seeking organisations and that it is too large and complex to be meaningful. In synthesising these issues, some have gone as far as to suggest the ethical consumer is a 'myth', as consumer decision-making is entirely context specific and based on complex individual trade-offs (Devinney et al., 2010). Others such as Heath and Potter (2006) argue that ethical consumption is not an answer in itself to the world's social and environmental problems anyway, due to its 'voluntariness'. These issues will be explored further in the final chapter of this book.

Schwartz (2010) notes that a consequence of difficulties in regulating business practices which might be considered to be ethically problematic is the emergence of citizens questioning whether they could be culpable for any unethical practices associated with their purchases, and whether a moral conscience can be expressed through purchasing choices.

We believe, as Miller (2012) notes, human beings *are* moral beings with moral choices often displayed in an obligation to others, and as Cova and Cova (2012) suggest, consumers are connected to society through their choices, assuming responsibility and its associated risks for themselves and others. As Schwartz (2010) argues therefore, consumers *can* be morally culpable for what they purchase. The remainder of this book will therefore explore the evidence on ethical consumption to address the complex landscape in which this purchasing occurs.

3 Segmentation perspectives on ethical consumption

As noted in the introduction, our first area of focus will be those studies which characterise early (and ongoing) research into ethical consumption which we classify under the heading of 'segmentation perspectives'. We will examine two subsets of studies: in the first subset, researchers have attempted to apply traditional marketing segmentation techniques to ethical consumption; that is, those which attempt to discover *who* ethical consumers are (for example, their personal sociodemographic, psychographic, behavioural or other traits). Early studies in particular, recognising increasing consumer demands for social responsibility, framed the issue largely as a market segmentation issue. Consequently, these applied demographic, socio-economic and psycho-social variables to understand who were the ethical consumers. The second subset includes studies which attempt to understand the ethical *motivations* of consumer groups. These have sought to understand the attitudes and motivations of ethical consumer groups, with a focus on the 'likelihood' of ethical purchase. Most of the studies in this category refer to proactive 'positive purchasing' behaviour (often in relation to Fair Trade or organic products), and the aim is to assess the size and shape of consumer intentions to purchase ethical products and services.

Regarding the first of these subsets of literature, Anderson and Cunningham (1972, p.23) were perhaps the first to recognise that in response to increasing consumer demands for social responsibility: "... the issue has shifted from one of corporate social responsibility to a more conventional market segmentation problem." Indeed, an early and continuing aspect of the ethical consumption literature is segmentation based. Anderson and Cunningham (1972) attempted to discover who socially conscious consumers were by segmenting by demographic and socio-psychological (levels of social consciousness) variables. They found that those with a higher social consciousness possessed certain characteristics (that is, they were likely to be in higher-status occupations,

DOI: 10.4324/9781003246954-3

with above average socio-economic status, more cosmopolitan and less conservative in outlook), but that there were not any statistically significant relationships across a number of variables, namely income, educational attainment and stage in the family life cycle.

Segmentation by demographic characteristics

As Hassan et al. (2021) note in their review of research into consumer ethical behaviour, personal, cultural and situational factors affect consumer ethical judgement, with the majority of articles (82.5%) exploring personal factors in consumer ethics research. Indeed, many studies have attempted to demonstrate links between various 'profile' characteristics and ethical motivation, as shown in Table 3.1:

These studies tend to conclude that these characteristics are important predictors of consumer ethical motivations and attitudes, although there is some inconsistency of results, as we will demonstrate.

Age

As Straughan and Roberts (1999) observed, age has been the subject of a range of studies since the early identification of green marketing. They argued that at that time it was generally considered that younger

Table 3.1 Examples of profile characteristics as determinants of ethical consumption

Profile characteristic as determinant of ethical consumption	Example studies
Age	Jayawardhena et al., 2016; Ha-Brookshire and Norum, 2011; De Pelsmacker et al., 2005
Gender	Pinna, 2019; Jayawardhena et al., 2016; Shang and Peloza, 2016; Pinto, et al., 2014; Hawkins, 2012; Ha-Brookshire and Norum, 2011
Religion/Religiosity	Ramasamy et al. 2010; Cornwell et al., 2005
Religiosity	Agag and Colmekcioglu, 2020; Alsaad et al., 2020; Chowdhury, 2020; Arli and Pekerti, 2017
Culture	Kim et al., 2010; Luedicke et al., 2009; Kozinets and Handelman, 1998; Vitell and Paolillo, 2004
Nationality	Arli and Pekerti, 2017; Babakus et al., 2004; Sims and Gegez, 2004

individuals were likely to be more environmentally sensitive, although they point to the lack of consistency in research at that date on this issue (as distinct from the field of consumer ethics, which typically finds that consumers become more ethical as they get older [see, for example, Moores and Chang, 2006; Rawwas and Singhapakdi, 1998]). Indeed, as Jayawardhena et al. (2016) argue, relationships between age and ethicality are long-established, with an assumption that the older a consumer is, the more likely they are to ascribe to ethical values. However, De Pelsmacker et al. (2005) found that attitudes towards Fair Trade products were stronger in the 31–44 years age bracket, and aligned to much public discourse about the prevalence of pro-social and pro-environmental awareness in younger people (Petro, 2020). Ha Brookshire and Norum (2011) found that younger people were more willing to pay more for ethical products, and more recent studies suggest that younger consumers (and 'Generation Z' [that is, those born between 1997 and 2012] in particular) have a strong awareness of and desire towards ethical and environmental issues (Djafarova and Foots, 2022; Robichaud and Yu, 2021), although as noted by Jayawardhena et al. (2016), this may be moderated by economic constraints, particularly for the purchase of organic and Fair Trade products, which may carry a price premium. Nevertheless, as noted by McKinsey's (Francis and Hoefl, 2018) *True Gen* report on Generation Z and implications for companies, they find that this generation is well-educated about brands and expect them to 'take a stand' on relevant causes and act with consistency and integrity on those causes.

Gender and gender identity

De Pelsmacker et al. (2005) found no significant differences between the sexes in relation to willingness to buy Fair Trade products, yet Fair Trade products have since become more widely available in a broader range of product categories. Additionally, the gender pay gap gradually narrowed in the intervening years and therefore the situation may subsequently have altered. Later research tends to indicate nuances between the ways in which ethical consumption between different genders may be perceived. For instance, Hawkins (2012) investigated the relationship between gender and Cause-Related Marketing (CRM), arguing that ethical consumption is by its very nature a gendered act, since at the time of her publication most household purchases were made by women. Furthermore, women were viewed stereotypically as being empathetic and therefore more likely than men to be targeted by ethically oriented marketing campaigns, with women and children depicted in specific CRM promotions, thus creating a gender-biased appeal

(Hawkins, 2012). However, the sources referred to here are indicative of a limitation of research into ethical consumption in that it tends to take a traditional male/female approach to gender by default, rarely incorporating non-binary perspectives. For example, Shang and Peloza (2016) found an unintended consequence of ethical purchasing was that it was perceived to be more a female than a male activity, although as in many studies in this field, the observers were limited to students and therefore were not necessarily representative of the wider population. Pinto et al. (2014) also highlighted a tendency for female respondents to engage in ethical consumption to a higher extent than male participants, yet when social identity was more salient rather than from a personal perspective, females and males were broadly equal in ethical purchase intention, thus advocating appeals to social groups for more effective promotional messaging. Similarly, Pinna (2019) highlights a number of areas of research which suggest that women are more likely to be concerned about social and environmental issues than men and are also more likely to be involved in pro-environmental behaviours and practice ethical consumption. However, Pinna (2019) further notes that these studies tend to be based on biological sex distinctions, and that very little research has approached ethical consumption in relation to gender identity. Here, gender identity is defined as the extent to which an individual identifies themselves with masculine or feminine personality traits. Pinna finds that (in young Italian consumers), regardless of gender, femininity (measured by feelings such as tenderness or sensitivity to others) significantly increases ethical intent, and it is therefore gender identity, not gender, that drives ethical intentions.

Religiosity, culture and nationality

Religiosity has been identified as one of the key cultural factors which can influence ethical consumption decisions. For example, in the context of choosing to stay at 'green' (that is, eco-efficient) hotels, Agag and Colmekcioglu (2020) found that Islamic religiosity influenced ethical purchase decisions, driven by subjective norms (that is, the belief that groups of people will support a specific behaviour). In another study on Muslim consumers, Alsaad et al. (2020) advocated the use of messages with religious appeals within religious societies, to discourage unethical consumption behaviour. Similarly, in a predominantly Christian sample group, Chowdhury (2020) found that religiosity had a positive influence on ethical consumption. Additionally, social appeals to consumers have been recommended as effective in Confucian cultures, particularly those based on close relationships (Chen and Moosmayer, 2018). Arli and Pekerti (2017) investigated ethical consumption further, comparing samples of consumers in Indonesia and Australia, discovering that culture was more of a dominant factor on certain ethical actions such as recycling, whereas religiosity had a stronger influence on the avoidance of negative consumer behaviour. The definition and application of morals are frequently referred to in research exploring religion and culture in relation to ethical consumption. Luedicke et al. (2009) considered ethical consumption as an integral component of contemporary culture, offering perspectives from interviewees which demonstrate the potentially subjective nature of ethics in terms of 'brand-mediated moral conflict', with two types of consumer (Hummer vehicle owners and non-Hummer drivers), each group viewing their own consumption behaviour as being ethical.

The impact of culture and/or nationality is covered inherently within many of the studies referred to in this section and it is noteworthy that ethical standards and norms can differ between countries, as evidenced in research by Vitell and Paolillo (2004). Babakus et al. (2004) concur, after assessing differences in the nature of unethical behaviour in six countries (Austria, Brunei, France, Hong Kong, the UK and the USA), concluding that when entering new international markets, companies must conduct research to gain insights into consumer behaviour in each country and not make assumptions about perceptions of ethical or unethical behaviour. Kim et al. (2010) also made cross-cultural comparisons between the USA and Korea, attributing the differences in behaviour in the context of Fair Trade brand loyalty to individualistic and collectivistic cultures in the respective countries. Offering a broader perspective on the actors within ethical consumption, Hawkins (2012) identified the Global North as generally being the purchasers and the Global South as beneficiaries of ethical consumption.

Demographic characteristics: summary

What can we summarise from these studies which aim to find out who the ethical consumers are? The reality perhaps is they are both everywhere and nowhere. Ethical consumers can be found in all definable demographic market segments, but at the same time it can be difficult to identify them according to these discrete characteristics. Indeed, many authors have argued that such demographic profiling is inherently unstable and that psychographic criteria (Straughan and Roberts, 1999), ethical motivation (McGoldrick and Freestone, 2008) or values (De Pelsmacker et al., 2005) provide the most effective basis for profiling ethical consumer behaviour. Devinney et al. (2010, p.8) go so far as to argue that predictive demographic characteristics are 'simplistic' and 'prove unfounded'. Indeed, it is likely that such simplistic models of causation cannot account for the complex contexts in which ethical decision-making is likely to occur.

Further, the evidence is that ethical consumers are rarely consistent with consumption habits varying across product and service types at different times and in relation to other pressing concerns. Compounding this are difficulties around identifying who is an 'ethical consumer'. Is somebody who always tries to prioritise buying Fair Trade coffee and bananas but rarely takes other ethical considerations into account in their other consumption decisions an ethical consumer? What is clear perhaps is that the individuals defined earlier in this book as ethical consumers hold particular values, and whilst these values may correspond with other psychographic variables (religiosity or social consciousness, for example), there are no clear links between those who hold those values and other demographic or socio-economic characteristics. We would therefore propose that ethical consumers exist on a spectrum or continuum, across which they may move during different life stages as their own characteristics and external influences fluctuate with time (see also Hiller and Woodall, 2019). Consumers may consequently make ethical purchase decisions some of the time and to varying extents, rather than behaving consistently in binary categories (for example, classified into ethical or unethical consumers) or segments. For example, McDonald et al. (2012) categorised certain consumers as 'selectors', as they make ethical decisions for certain products or service purchases, such as food, yet not for selecting other items, which can change incrementally over time.

Segmentation by ethical motivation

Bridging the two groups of studies are segmentation models of ethical consciousness or motivation, such as those described in early studies, including those of Schlegelmilch et al. (1996) and Cowe and Williams (in Nicholls and Opal, 2005). The former finds that environmental consciousness may impact purchasing decisions, although other moderating factors may also be at play. The latter classified UK consumers into five segments (also drawing on sociodemographic factors) with a suggested market share (represented in brackets): Global Watchdogs (5%), Brand Generation (6%), Conscientious Consumers (18%), Look after My Own (22%) and Do What I Can (49%). Whilst the research was based on a reasonably limited intercept sample of 2000, Nicholls and Opal (2005) argue that the segments which offer the most potential growth for ethical products and services are the 'Global Watchdogs' and 'Conscientious Customers', with the 'Do What I Cans' also 'showing promise'.

Similarly, the UK Government Department for Environment, Food and Rural Affairs (DEFRA), as part of their drive to improve sustainable consumption practices in the late 2000s, also developed a segmentation model to show the ability and willingness of the population at large to adopt the behaviour changes DEFRA identified as part of their drive towards greater sustainability (DEFRA, 2008). Supporting this model was a segmentation framework to better understand how approaches can be tailored for different groups. The environmental segmentation model (ESM) identified seven clusters, each representing a distinct set of attitudes and beliefs towards the environment, environmental issues and behaviours, including ecological worldview, socio-geodemographics, lifestyle, attitudes towards behaviours and current behaviours, motivations and barriers, and knowledge and engagement (DEFRA, 2008). These segments were also considered in terms of their ability to act but were not restricted to those proactive consumers identified as 'ethically motivated' and covered a sample of the entire (UK) population, including those that may be reactive or not ethically aware/motivated. Three segments contained the most willing to act and had relatively high potential to do more. Segment one (Positive Greens) could be considered to be comparable to Cowe and Williams' 'Global Watchdogs', and segment-three consumers (Concerned Consumers) are broadly similar to 'Conscientious Consumers' in that their environmental views are less strong, but this is one aspect of their personality and possible derived value. Drawing these parallels, it is interesting to note that the percentages of the population attributed to each segment are reasonably consistent, except with those at the 'top end' of ethical motivation, with DEFRA's 'Positive Greens' accounting for 18% and Cowe and Williams' 'Global Watchdogs' only 5% (which could be accounted for changes occurring in the eight-year period between the studies). It should be noted that neither model addresses the question of whether consumers might fall under different classifications in terms of their likelihood to respond to different issues, and it could be argued that these models should not be considered as one- or two-dimensional frameworks as there may be other variables which overlap, or they may be time or circumstance specific.

Applying a 'best–worst' study, Burke et al. (2014) further segment consumers according to their reasons for choosing or rejecting ethical products, finding that whilst many consumers wish to make a difference and do care about ethical issues, barriers related to confusion and scepticism remain. They also find that reasons for or against ethical purchasing were more likely to relate to issues of well-being or health, rather than for reasons of social concerns (such as status or fitting in with peers).

Consumer attitudes towards ethical consumption

The second sub-field of literature under this perspective has sought to understand the attitudes and motivations of ethical consumer groups, with a focus on the 'likelihood' of ethical purchase. Most of these studies refer to proactive *positive purchasing* behaviour and often in relation to Fair Trade or organic products, although it is recognised that such behaviour only comprises one of the many ways in which consumers may exhibit ethical behaviour (Harrison et al., 2005). In 'early' studies, the stated importance of ethics appeared to be relatively high. For example, Creyer and Ross (1997) presented the results of a survey of US consumers' attitudes to ethical behaviour which claimed that ethics was an important purchase consideration and consumers will reward those organisations seen as ethical by a willingness to pay higher prices and punish those which are not seen as ethical, not necessarily by not purchasing, but by wanting to purchase at lower prices (it is important to note that ethical and unethical behaviours were not specified in this study). Kim et al. (1999) presented one of the first studies directly related to clothing in which they examined the relative importance of socially responsible attitudes, alongside catalogue shopping involvement and product-related attributes, as predictors of consumers' intentions to purchase clothing. Similarly to Creyer and Ross (1997), they concluded that social responsibility is an important predictor in purchase intention, although desire for individuality exerts the greatest influence. As can be seen, some of these earlier studies of ethical consumption tend towards the 'optimistic'; ethical concerns are generally seen to be of importance to consumers (although not necessarily *the* most important as highlighted by Creyer and Ross, 1997). Indeed, Connolly and Shaw (2006) argued that research suggests consumer concern for ethical issues was increasing at that time, and Shaw et al. (2006, p.439) argue that: "Consumers are calling for ethical products to be available on the high street... ." Indeed, since that time retailers have responded and it has now become the norm for most retailers in the UK to include a selection of products labelled as 'eco' or 'sustainable', albeit often without a clear definition of how the items meet these credentials.

The results of Littrell et al. (2005) survey also show that despite generational differences with regard to political and social attitudes and style, quality and value in clothing "...all groups held strong views related to Fair Trade ideology and global responsibility" (p.415). Hyllegard et al.'s (2009) quantitative study of 'Generation Y' consumers' attitudes to Fair Trade advertising messages in the clothing industry finds that attitudes towards advertisements communicating fair labour principles are more positive than those using sex to sell the products. Mohr and Webb (2005) find that consumers value CSR and this is an important factor in purchase decisions regardless of product parity or price, and Schlegelmilch et al. (1996) find that environmental awareness *may* impact on consumers' purchase decisions (although note that other moderating factors are likely to be significant). Other studies have continued this theme. For example, Schröder and McEachern (2004) examine ethical attitudes towards animal welfare standards in food purchase; Cailleba and Casteran (2010) examine customer loyalty in the purchase of Fair Trade coffee; Ha-Brookshire and Norum (2011) find that over half of their respondents were willing to pay more for US-grown organic or sustainable cotton shirts and Ma et al. (2012) find that young females possess positive attitudes towards buying Fair Trade products. Davies et al. (2012) examine different product types and find that ethics is more likely to be a consumer concern in commodities than for luxury goods.

These studies are based, often through the use of surveys, on questioning respondents' attitudes, and these studies consequently make recommendations to the marketers of 'ethical' products. However, four issues arise: firstly, as Strong (1997) notes, there are a number of problems in encouraging consumers to buy 'ethically'. Whilst these problems are focused on Fair Trade principles, they may have 'equivalence' to other ethical concerns. They are problems in communicating the human (rather than environmental) element of sustainability, consumer commitment to the cause and consistency in buying behaviour, and the availability of Fair Trade products. Second is the gap between stated attitudes and actual behaviour. Worcester and Dawkins (2005) point to MORI research, which suggests that the public claim to be concerned about ethical issues in buying products and services, but stress that there is a marked gap between attitude and action and that "...consumer behaviour lags behind the stated level of concern about ethical issues" (as previously stated, they argue that this is largely due to the ineffective communication of ethical issues to consumers). The third issue relates to the research methods used in studies of ethical consumption. There are two considerations here. First is the likelihood of social desirability bias (this will be examined in more detail in Chapter 5, but highlights the likely unwillingness of individuals to 'confess' to holding unethical attitudes). Also, the studies of the ethical concerns of consumers in the clothing market highlighted above are based upon narrow samples or are contradictory. For example, studies by Davies et al. (2012) and Ma et al. (2012) and many others are based upon samples of university students and it could be argued that students are potentially more informed and politicised with regard to issues of ethics (Hyllegard et al., 2009). Studies of the 'general' consumer are inconclusive; studies of Iwanow et al. (2005) and Littrell et al. (2005) are based upon convenience samples of mail survey or shopping centre customers, but the former finds that ethics is not an important concern whereas the latter finds that ethics is an important dimension of customer wants, although as previously discussed these wants will not necessarily be translated into actions. Fourth, these heavily statistically driven surveys are often based on objective assumptions around tightly defined normative characterisations of ethics. That is, 'ethicality' is defined from a range of desirable or undesirable actions which are defined and tested through the use of quantitative scales, whereas as the previous chapter demonstrated, morality is much more likely to be subjectively determined, pluralistic and fluid, and correspondingly the more relevant challenge for consumer researchers in this field is to explore individual moral consciousness as a basis for decision-making.

A number of studies have therefore emerged which have aimed to estimate the potential size of ethical markets and make recommendations to marketers by testing respondents' attitudes towards particular ethical issues. As this summary indicates, there are a number of additional problems and pitfalls highlighted by these studies. The remaining chapters aim to examine these in more detail: to challenge some of the claims made and examine the more critical approach which has emerged in recent years.

4 Psychological perspectives on ethical consumption

Following the segmentation perspectives outlined in the previous chapter, a second major area of literature seeks to understand ethical consumption largely from a 'psychological' perspective, positioning the ethical consumer as a rational decision-maker. We argue that these studies may be considered to be a 'second wave' of ethical consumption research, characterising much of the research in the late 1990s and early part of the twentieth century onwards. These studies tend to fall into one of two broad fields: those utilising expectancy-value models and those utilising 'moral norm' or value-belief models.

Expectancy-value models consider the costs and benefits of particular (ethical) behaviours (expectancy) and weigh them against personal values, with those behaviours resulting in the greatest net benefit or utility being chosen on the basis that societal utility is maximised when individual utility is maximised, leading to positive outcomes (Cohen, 1972). These are often also based on 'deontological' (that is, an ethics based on duty) moral norms about the right thing to do (de Groot et al., 2016). There has been a significant focus within the consumer behaviour and business ethics literature on such consequentialist decision-making process models and many of the earlier (and continuing) studies are characterised by this approach, most notably underpinned by the Theory of Reasoned Action (TRA; Fishbein and Ajzen, 2010) and the Theory of Planned Behaviour (TPB; Ajzen, 1991). Many studies of ethical choice have explored the roles of ethical obligation and self-identity or other profile characteristics in applying these models to ethical consumption, or to understand the gap between ethical intentions and behaviour (for example, Djafarova and Foots, 2022; Pinna, 2019; Sreen et al., 2018; Lu et al., 2015).

The 'moral norms' approach is focused on a consumer altruism (see Thøgersen, 1996) which assumes a purposeful ethical 'awakening' that might lead to pro-environmental choices and behaviours (de Groot

DOI: 10.4324/9781003246954-4

et al., 2016). Stern (2000) calls this 'value-belief norm theory' and, as with others of this tradition, grounds ideas in the typological work of Schwartz (1994) and Rokeach (1973). Both acknowledge that values can be ascribed in two different ways: as terminal values (or preferred end states) set as overall goals for a successful life, or as instrumental values that act as guiding principles, orienting the consumer towards behaviours likely to facilitate those goals. These latter are sometimes expressed as virtues such as moderation, practical wisdom and constancy (Garcia-Ruiz and Rodriquez-Lluesma, 2014). It is suggested, therefore, that a link exists between 'good' – or morally oriented personal values – and ethics and behaviour, and this reflects a widely held view that values are central to consumer actions (see, for example, Chowdhury, 2020; Manchiraju and Sadachar, 2014; Shaw et al., 2005). Both these approaches are worthy of further consideration, given their prominence in research into ethical consumption.

Expectancy-value models: the theories of reasoned action and planned behaviour

As noted earlier, many studies of ethical consumers (for example, Sun, 2019; Shaw et al., 2000) and ethical consumption (for example, Djafarova and Foots, 2022) have employed the TRA and TPB to explain and predict ethical consumer behaviour (see, Han and Stoel, 2017, for a meta-analytic review). Fishbein and Ajzen (2010) present a brief chronology of the development of the TPB and TRA, noting that they first proposed the TRA in 1980. The TRA attempted to link attitudes with behaviour in order to allow a prediction of behaviour and to enable an understanding of how to change behaviour (that is, the purpose of the TRA is to try to explain or predict behaviour). Fishbein and Ajzen (2010) note that this could be in many domains, but focus principally on organisational, political and discriminatory behaviours. Researchers have since applied the model widely to the study of consumer behaviour. The TRA was based on Fishbein's earlier expectancy-value model, which proposed that an individual's attitude is determined by beliefs about the likely outcomes of performing a particular behaviour (known as behavioural beliefs), weighted by the individual's evaluations of those outcomes. Added to this was the 'subjective norm', which represents the pressure the perceived views of others exert on engaging in a behaviour. The TRA also included 'background' factors such as demographics, personality traits and other individual variables. After a brief diversion of careers, Ajzen then added the construct of 'perceived behavioural control' to account for the notion that an individual would be aware of factors which may enable or prevent the behaviour.

The TRA proposes that intention is the most important predictor of behaviour, and this is influenced by combinations of attitudinal (positive or negative evaluations of engaging in the behaviour), normative (social pressure) and control (ability to engage in the behaviour, or *self-efficacy*) considerations. Behavioural, normative and control beliefs are underpinned by a variety of 'background' factors grouped as individual (including both the values previously discussed and the profile characteristics discussed in Chapter 3), social or information factors.

In an early study, Sparks and Shepherd (1992) applied the model to the study of 'green consumers' and found that the role of 'self-identity' is also important as a separate construct from attitude in applying the TRA to 'moral considerations'. Self-identity here is contrasted to attitude or behaviour by the following line of thought: "I would enjoy doing A, and I think I should do A (or B), but I am the type of person more oriented to doing C" (Biddle et al., in Sparks and Shepherd, 1992, p.389). The inclusion of self-identity is also supported by Shaw et al. (2000) and Hustvedt and Dickson (2009). Bartels and Onwezen (2014) further recognise the potential role of social identity in shaping intentions to purchase, or those who identify with a particular group of consumers, in their case consumers of organic products. In the case of the former, again, the self-identity reported here is characterised by the 'rational agent', one who plans and has an integrated and consistent sense of self. It is recognised that this perspective may be limiting, and alternative perspectives on self-identity will be explored in the next chapter. Sun (2019) also argues that self-identity as it is conceptualised in studies of ethical consumption is separate to ethical concerns and thus disconnected from moral identity. Shaw et al. (2000) further note that in addition to self-identity, many authors have also argued for the inclusion of 'ethical obligation': "…an individual's internalised ethical rules, which reflect their personal beliefs about right and wrong" (p.882). Ethical obligation thus relates to an individual's 'internalised' personal moral beliefs or values. Shaw et al. (2000) argue that these two additional factors (self-identity and ethical obligation) are more significant factors than attitude and subjective norm in making ethical purchases. Significantly, both self-identity and ethical obligation are closely related to an individual's values, and there is likely be a strong conceptual link between the values identified in the TRA and self-identity and ethical obligation.

However, the TRA has been claimed to be limited in its application to the total consumption process for a number of reasons. Firstly, as

Shaw et al. (2000) note, models such as the TRA are more suited to self-interested behaviours and may be deficient in explaining ethical or moral motivations. Following from this, it is also not guaranteed that maximising individual utility will result in optimal aggregate outcomes. Secondly, it assumes that a consumer's intentions to purchase are consistent with ethical judgement (Chatzidakis et al., 2006). Thirdly, Sheppard et al. (1988) note that the TRA is only effective when the subject has full control over a particular behaviour. However, a lack of information or ability to make a particular purchase could arguably lead to loss of control, and more widely the TRA is based on a series of assumptions about human agency, and whilst the TPB addresses this through the addition of behavioural control, there are further implications of this in relation to the proclaimed 'attitude–behaviour gap' which will be explored in Chapter 6. Finally, Sun (2019) argues that confidence (perceived certainty regarding in personal judgements about an outcome) is the key moderating factor in the relationship between attitudes and intentions in ethical consumption, but that this factor was disregarded by the architect of the TPB.

Value-belief/moral norm models

Partly in response to some of the shortcomings highlighted earlier, a second set of literature drawing on psychological perspectives has focused on deontologically based moral norms (Thøgersen, 1996) and value theory. In an environmental-behaviour setting, Stern (2000) has termed this 'value-belief norm theory', and along with others has grounded this in the values-based work of Schwartz (1994) and Rokeach (1973). As noted earlier, this recognises that there is an inherent link between an individual's values and both their ethics and their behaviour, and presumes a purposeful ethical 'awakening' that might lead to pro-environmental behaviours. Indeed, it is widely accepted that values constitute a central influence which determines consumers' consumption behaviours, and Smith (1999) argues that the role of values is essential in differentiating between consumption behaviour, which may be considered to be 'wrong', and consumer behaviour, which is a deliberate attempt to do good. As Jägel et al. (2012) and Shaw et al. (2005) note, values serve as guiding principles and therefore play a significant role in determining ethical consumption, and studies in ethical consumption have consequently adopted this perspective (see, for example, Manchiraju and Sadachar, 2014; de Groot and Steg, 2010).

The role of values

As noted earlier, the development of the concept of values is perhaps influenced most by Schwartz (1994) and Rokeach (1973), who defines a value as "… an enduring belief that a specific mode of conduct or end-state of existence is personally or socially preferable to an opposite or converse mode of conduct or state of existence" (p.5). Therefore, values can be concerned with modes of conduct (instrumental values) or desirable end states of existence (terminal values). In ethical consumption, these latter are sometimes expressed as virtues such as moderation (for example, Garcia-Ruiz and Rodriquez-Lluesma, 2014). It is therefore suggested that a link exists between 'good' or morally oriented personal values, ethics and behaviour, and this reflects the widely held view that values are central to consumers' consumption behaviours. According to Rokeach (1973), terminal values may be personal (self-centred or intrapersonal, but also perhaps relating to 'peace of mind') or social (society-centred or interpersonal). Instrumental values consist of moral values (a narrow conception which relates to modes of behaviour and the types of values related to interpersonal instrumental values which have the potential to arouse guilt for wrongdoing) and competence values (self-actualisation values not related to morality but rather shame due to personal inadequacy, for example). The notion of 'end states' is thus an important one; Baudrillard (1998) notes that products serve a practical purpose but act as elements of 'higher-order' states which have social meanings attached, such as prestige or comfort. He argues that the field of consumption relates to these higher-order states, rather than the product features which relate to its use.

Gutman (1982) notes that the achievement of terminal values may often be a subconscious process and therefore identifies three levels of distinctions: values (end states of existence), consequences (outcomes for the consumer) and grouping (product attributes and grouping them with similar products). These levels are linked to behaviour through the means–end chain, which aims to explain how the attributes of different product or service choices facilitate the achievement of end states, or terminal values. Zeithaml (1988) proposes that means–end chains allow a differentiation of different levels of abstraction, from product attributes through to value levels (where instrumental values precede terminal values). It has been argued that means–end theory is the most effective explanation of consumers' buying behaviour (see, for example, Paul et al., 2009 and Zeithaml, 1988), and correspondingly some studies in ethical consumption have therefore applied means–end approaches. Jägel et al. (2012), for example, have applied a means–end chain approach to ethical clothing consumption in which they find that although they consider coding the complexities problematic within the hierarchical value maps, value for money and style conflict with ethical concerns, resulting in 'value trade-offs'.

Complexity in choice is often given as a reason for the existence of an ethical consumption 'attitude–behaviour gap'. Gutman argues that when faced with complexity, consumer thinking is managed via 'categorisation processes' through which consumers group products or services by features which are emphasised or ignored. Some retailers have addressed this through 'choice-editing' strategies such as offering Fair Trade–only ranges). Whilst the grouping is based on the properties (or features) of the product or service, those properties focused upon are influenced by terminal values. More widely, in their seminal work on 'service-dominant logic' in marketing, Vargo and Lusch (2004, 2008) argue that the importance of the achievement of higher-order benefits through the purchase of goods has increased, and that these needs are often associated with the provision of satisfaction. Schwartz (1994, p.20) summarises these perspectives by noting that there is a widespread agreement that values share five conceptual features: firstly, that a value is a belief, and secondly that these beliefs relate to desirable end states (terminal values) or modes of conduct (instrumental values). Thirdly, values transcend specific situations, and fourthly they "...guide selection or evaluation of behaviour, people and events." Finally, values are ordered in terms of relative importance to form a system of value priorities.

Rokeach (1973) identifies a number of characteristics of values which are of importance: firstly, values are enduring as they are taught or learned to be absolute, but they are also relative in that values may be ordered in terms of importance in situations where several values may compete (and so they 'assist' in conflict resolution and decision-making). Secondly, a value is a belief upon which one acts through choice and which has cognitive, affective and behavioural (conative) components. Thirdly, values are versatile; they may be shared or not shared, applied to oneself or others, or they may be employed as double standards. The relationships between these values can be characterised by the value system, which Rokeach (1973) defines as "...an enduring organisation of beliefs concerning preferable modes of conduct or end-states of existence along a continuum of relative importance" (p.5). Rokeach notes that a variety of theorists have placed the total number of terminal values an individual may possess between 2 and 28, with several times that number of instrumental values, although he proposes a list of 18 instrumental and terminal values.

Whilst several authors have rejected Rokeach's values as not relating closely enough to most of life's major roles, including consumption (Bloemer and Dekker, 2007; Kahle and Kennedy, 1988), Schwartz (1994) notes that few of the attempts to classify values have gained wide acceptance and further argues that Rokeach's classifications of values are all conceptually very different with little empirical correlation. He adds a further dimension to the characteristics of values by noting the importance of motivation requirements of individuals; that values represent *conscious* goals which respond to the universal needs of humans (he cites these requirements as being biological needs [organism], needs related to social interaction [interaction] and needs related to the effectiveness and survival of groups [group]). Thus, values motivate action and function as standards for judging and justifying action. The prominence of motivation is significant; according to Schwartz (2009), in researching values researchers who overlook this factor often confound values and attitudes, with implications for the validity of values research. Schwartz therefore defines value types in terms of a central goal (similar to terminal values), with a classification of values that represent each type (similar to instrumental values) and the requirements from which each value type is derived as in Table 4.1. Schwartz argues these values are applicable across all cultures and many researchers have utilised Schwartz's values and value meanings to explore the role of values in ethical consumption (see, for example, Shaw et al., 2005).

Problems with values

However, an important aspect of this is to recognise that, as proposed by Firat et al. (1995), contemporary consumers are increasingly fickle and unpredictable, and that whilst values take time to change, they do change and, perhaps more significantly: "… [consumers] often subscribe to highly contradictory value systems, lifestyles etc., concurrently, without feeling inconsistent and improper" (p.44). Indeed, Schwartz (1994) notes that the pursuit of values has consequences that may conflict with the pursuit of other value types, and he goes on to observe that it is the relative importance of multiple values which guides action. Likewise, Brown (2006, p.226) claims "…the phenomenon known as the postmodern consumer, which comprises gendered subject positions indulging in playful combinations of contrasting identities, roles and characters (each with its requisite regalia of consumables) is now an accepted, if under-investigated, socio-cultural artifact…". Firat and Venkatesh (1995) argue that the 'postmodern consumer' is characterised

Table 4.1 Schwartz's motivational types of values

Definition	Exemplary values	Sources
Power: social status and prestige, control or dominance over people and resources.	Social power, authority, wealth.	Interaction Group
Achievement: personal success through demonstrating competence according to social standards.	Successful, capable, ambitious.	Interaction Group
Hedonism: pleasure and sensuous gratification for oneself.	Pleasure, enjoying life.	Organism
Stimulation: excitement, novelty and challenge in life.	Daring, varied life, exciting life.	Organism
Self-direction: independent thought and action – choosing, creating, exploring.	Creativity, curious, freedom.	Organism Interaction
Universalism: understanding, appreciation, tolerance and protection for the welfare of all people and for nature.	Broad-minded, social justice, equality.	Group Organism
Benevolence: preservation and enhancement of the welfare of people with whom one is in frequent personal contact.	Helpful, honest, forgiving.	Organism Interaction Group
Tradition: respect, commitment and acceptance of the customs and ideas that traditional culture or religion provide.	Humble, devout. Accepting my portion in life.	Group
Conformity: restraint of actions, inclinations and impulses likely to upset or harm others and violate social expectations or norms.	Politeness, obedient, honouring parents and elders.	Interaction Group
Security: safety, harmony and stability of society, of relationships and of self.	National security, social order, clean.	Organism Interaction Group

Source: Schwartz, 1994, p.22.

by two conditions: fragmentation and decentredness. Fragmentation describes the emancipation of the consumer from market forces as he or she engages in 'multiple consumption experiences' in an attempt to restructure his or her identity. Decentredness aims to capture the consumer in the context of individual everyday life, rather than through the 'lens of unifying theories'; that is, that multiple and possibly contradictory values, emotions and cognition could be held simultaneously by consumers, leading to diversity in consumer choices (Firat and Venkatesh, 1995). This is supported to some degree by the research into ethical consumer behaviour. For example, Joergens (2006) notes that consumers may possess ethical motivation but may not act ethically if products do not meet other important criteria. Valor (2007) highlights the central category of 'ambivalence' in ethical (clothing) purchase; a condition of arousal that occurs when an individual's values are inconsistent. Further, Devinney et al. (2010) argue that the scales on which most values research are based are flawed and lack validity because they work on an assumption that context does not 'interact' with values, and that given values are difficult to change, consumer research focused on behaviour change employing 'traditional' values research relies on a "... religious conversion of sorts" (p.172).

Trade-offs

As argued in Hiller and Woodall (2019), the approaches described earlier are often concerned with trade-offs. The expectancy-values approach, for example, suggests consumers compare and contrast different options (attributes and/or functional consequences), rejecting some and prioritising others (de Groot et al., 2016). Similarly, as in the work of Schwartz (1994), values are said to be organised as integrated motivational systems, hierarchically sorted to guide and establish option priorities. In both cases, consumers are implicitly assumed to weigh the benefits and sacrifices of each opportunity and then act to achieve the best outcome. As previously demonstrated by Jägel et al. (2012), a more formal notion of trade-offs as discrete decision-making processes is also found significant in emerging evidence on ethical consumption (see also Luchs and Kumar, 2017; Ha-Brookshire and Norum, 2011). Such studies have sought to focus on trade-offs, exploring these via distinct case-specific scenarios that focus explicitly on competing options. Burke et al. (2014) and Devinney et al. (2010), for example, apply 'best–worst' experiments, in which consumers are asked to rate the relative importance of objects of conflicting perceptual difference and are asked to rate the trade-off. Glac (2009) similarly considers trade-offs involving different types of functional consequence (the results of investing in two different pension schemes), whilst Luchs and Kumar (2017) appraise contrasting merits of both aesthetic versus sustainable product attributes and utilitarian versus sustainable product attributes. As an alternative to best–worst comparisons, others suggest cost–benefit as relevant competing options. These focus often on how price influences consumers where virtuous options are marked higher than the competition (Lim et al., 2014; Abrantes Ferreira et al., 2010; De Pelsmacker et al., 2005).

The literature pertaining to trade-offs frequently positions these as conflicts that apply at a cognitive level of decision-making. Hassan et al. (2013) and Schröder and McEachern (2004), for example, describe contradictions that arise from guilt and the breaking of ethical rules; McGoldrick and Freestone (2008) argue that we accrue a 'balance sheet' of gains and losses that are in opposition and state consequently this represents a conflict to be resolved. Such conflicts have been described as representing 'difficult value judgements' or 'hard choices' (McShane et al., 2011; Moisander, 2007), whilst both Johnstone and Tan (2015) and Valor (2007) refer to the necessary compromises or sacrifices consumers need to make to consume in accordance with their values. The role of rational decision-making in settling such internal disputes is evident in these accounts, and all trade-offs invoked imply the consumer is engaged in an act of preferential judgement. In these judgements multiple factors are compared to arrive at a course of action which balances the relative importance of both the benefits and sacrifices of engaging in an act. This balancing of benefit and sacrifice is also a central strand within work relating to the concept of consumer perceived value (see, for example, Ng and Smith, 2012; Sanchez-Fernandez et al., 2009), itself considered to be one of (if not *the*) most fundamental concepts within the concept of marketing (Vargo and Lusch, 2012; Gallarza et al., 2011; Holbrook, 1994). These ideas, most notably explored by Heskett et al. (1994) and Zeithaml (1988), have given rise to the view that consumers are conditioned to make rational comparisons of the good and the bad in exchange relationships, and to choose the option delivering the greatest net benefit (value).

Psychological perspectives: summary

Studies focused on either expectancy-value or moral norms are a prominent feature of the ethical consumption research landscape and explain and utilise the three key elements underpinning mainstream research in ethical consumption: products and/or their attributes, consumption consequences and human (or corporate) values. Some authors have sought to combine expectancy-value and moral norm theories by proposing ethical obligation as an antecedent to intent (see, for example, Aertsens et al., 2009; Shaw et al., 2000). Indeed, as Holbrook (1994) notes, consumption is not merely utilitarian and that morality contributes substantially to the choices people make and ethical benefits can be derived from behaviours motivated beyond self-interest. However, as highlighted earlier, these cognitive and rational benefit/ sacrifice approaches have been called into question, and Gummerus

(2013) suggests these should be replaced, instead, by a 'phenomeno-logical value' (Helkulla et al., 2012); that is, a value that is rooted 'in-the-experience' (Tynan et al., 2014) or 'in-context' (Chandler and Vargo, 2011) and that emphasises value's multi-contextual and dynamic nature (Heinonen et al., 2013). More recent studies focusing on value as a balance between benefit and sacrifice have consequently focused on trade-off and experience as conjoined entities (for example, Hiller and Woodall, 2019; Luchs and Kumar, 2017). Indeed, as Vargo and Lusch (2012) note, value is *contextually specific* and contingent on the avail-ability and integration of other relevant resources; that is, that value is determined (or perhaps formed) through integrative processes that are not 'simple' *cognitive* trade-offs but which evolve within those structures where actors 'exist' and which can be both enabling and constraining. This leads us to the next area of focus for studies in ethical consump-tion: those which we define as 'sociological' perspectives.

5 Sociological perspectives on ethical consumption

In Chapter 4, we concluded by noting a growing rejection of approaches to ethical consumption which position the consumer as a rational decision-maker, engaged in conscious and deliberative trade-offs. Of course, rational information-processing models (including those related to trade-offs) are still employed in research into ethical consumption, but these studies are now considered just part of an evolving research tradition (for example, Moraes et al., 2012; Phipps et al., 2013) which represent a small, but prominent, dimension of ethical consumption research (Janssen and Vanhamme, 2015). As Caruana (2007) notes, such 'techno-rational' discourses focused entirely on what motivates consumers to buy overlook the social processes and meanings that may underpin the notion and nature of ethical or responsible consumption, and Schaefer and Crane (2005) and Jackson (2005) have critiqued cognitively bound thinking and have been influential in the development of an alternative focus on social and cultural backgrounds as a guide to behaviour. Whilst in similar critiques others have focused on the role of emotions and intuitions (see, for example, Zollo, 2021), in this chapter we will therefore focus on the 'third wave' of a growing number of studies of ethical consumption which identify the importance of relocating the consideration of ethical consumption (both individually and collectively) within the cultural ethics of consumption (Newholm and Shaw, 2007). That is, by considering consumption practices at a sociological level. Here ethical consumption is not considered to be exclusively the result of a process of self-inquiry; cultural backgrounds, personal histories and the social context are also critical (Cherrier, 2007; Jackson, 2005; Schaefer and Crane, 2005).

Caruana (2007) proposes three predominant sociological conceptions of morality: a classical view based on viewing patterns of consumption in relation to dominant social structures; a constructivist perspective, under which consumers attempt to use morality in part to develop an

DOI: 10.4324/9781003246954-5

identification of the self and social self; and a contemporary perspective, in which morality is complex and dynamic and entirely related to an individual's existential condition and their ability to self-determine right and good. In consumption, these sociological perspectives are largely reflected in the canon of work under the 'consumer culture theory' (CCT) banner (Arnould and Thompson, 2005), and two emergent strands of sociological thought have emerged under this perspective (Thompson et al., 2013). The first views consumption as a form of identity work (both personal and collective) and the 'lived world' of consumers (Arnould and Thompson, 2005), and the second relates to Caruana's (2007) classification of 'constructivist' sociological perspectives on consumption morality. Here, ethical consumption is viewed as a sociological practice, in which there is increased interest for the study of consumption (Halkier et al., 2011; Warde, 2005). As Corsini et al. (2019) find, work on consumer identity dominated the research field in the period 2009–2012, with practice theories beginning to dominate from 2015 onwards. We will therefore consider each of these perspectives: consumer identity projects and practice theories.

Consumer identity projects

Following from Belk's (1988) widely cited study, Arnould and Thompson (2005) noted that there was (and continues to be) increasing interest in how consumers use consumption-related activities to display their circumstances (personal and social) and further their identity goals. Consumer identity work has gained significant momentum in studies of consumption more generally, predicated on the notion that consumption is a (or even perhaps *the*) central function in human life and that consumers use products, services and brands as 'props' to self-identity (Arnould and Thompson, 2005; Belk, 1988). Devinney et al. (2010) argued that until that point, the role of the individual had been understated in research into ethical consumption in favour of the preoccupation with the segmentation techniques outlined in Chapter 3. Correspondingly, a body of research into ethical consumption has sought to understand how consumer identities are formed through a discourse of ethical consumption (see, for example, Bartels and Onwezen, 2014; Carrington et al., 2014; Luedicke et al., 2009). As Cherrier (2007) observes, ethical consumption practices emerge through the 'interplay' between not only individual but also collective identity and, as previously noted, self-identity has emerged as a key dimension in studies applying the TPB (see, for example, Udell et al., 2020; Hustvedt and Dickson, 2009; Shaw et al., 2000; Sparks and Shepherd, 1992).

Developing this assertion from sociological perspectives, as Shaw and Riach (2011) argue, the act of 'ethical consumption' should be distinguished from the position of 'being' an ethical consumer, and a number of studies of morality in consumption have adopted perspectives on identity, both at the level of the individual (see, for example, Luedicke et al., 2009; Cherrier, 2006) and in terms of social identity (Bartels and Onwezen, 2014). It has been increasingly recognised that consumer identity is fluid (Bauman, 2008; Cherrier and Murray, 2007), especially where ethical consumer 'subjectivities' are adapted in response to changing historical conditions (Giesler and Veresiu, 2014). As Bauman (2008) argues, identities (themselves processes of socialisation) exist in a continuous lifelong process of 'renegotiation'; at no stage are they final. Indeed, as previously noted, Firat and Venkatesh (1995) noted how postmodern consumer identities were restructured through participation in diverse consumption experiences. In response, Giesler and Veresiu (2014) encourage consumer researchers to consider not how cultural systems shape consumer identities, but how, for example, family and other social structures are rearticulated as consumption systems. Cherrier and Murray (2007) perhaps take a 'third way' with this and argue that identity construction is 'middle-out' in that at times consumers have the freedom to act as creative agents, and at others they are shaped by cultural and historical structures. There is therefore scope to explore these different, and potentially conflicting, perspectives on consumer identities, and the extent to which there is an influence of cultural structures, or whether social identities are reshaped as consumption systems. It should be noted that Bauman (2008) highlights a problem with the 'identity project' in its totality as it relates to ethical consumption: that the notion of responsible choice (perhaps once based on an ethics of duty and characterised by responsibility to the 'other') is now 'overshadowed' by responsibility to oneself, characterised by self-fulfilment and the calculation of risks. However, it remains a significant facet of the evidence related to factors underpinning ethical consumption practices, and this is worthy of further consideration.

One of the authors who has perhaps shaped perspectives on identity more than any others is Giddens (1991), who identifies a number of dimensions of identity which are relevant in an (ethical) consumption context. Firstly, he argues that identity is reflexive; we are not what we are, but what we make ourselves, with opportunities for individuals to establish identities and 'reinvent' themselves based on experience and reflection (as identified by Giesler and Veresiu, 2014); in this perspective (as noted by Hiller and Woodall, 2019), the 'ethical consumer' is an entity which exists, but which is never fully formed in the context of learning, development and changes in an individual's 'life project'. Other authors have sought to explore how ethical consumers may employ different strategies to avoid the negative effects on self-image that may arise from the guilt caused by disengaging from ethical acts (see, for example, Chatzidakis et al.'s, 2004 study on consumers' deployment of neutralisation techniques, or Carrington et al.'s 2015 research into the moral dilemmas which consumers attempt to reconcile in the development of a more coherent self). Secondly, Giddens argues that the self forms a trajectory of development from the past to an anticipated future, perhaps corresponding in part at least to the value-belief or moral norm models explored in Chapter 2. As Hiller and Woodall (2019) and Garcia-Ruiz and Rodriguez-Lluesma (2014) note, 'green' and ethical consumption practices do not occur in isolation but are part of an ongoing project of sustainable consumption that might involve different goals related to, for example, health, family, saving money, living more spiritually or achieving social justice. Thirdly, Giddens notes that the reflexivity of self extends to the body; here the body is seen as an action system and not just a passive object. Pecoraro et al. (2021) extend this idea to focus on other embodied aspects of consumption which employ all of the senses to interpret ethical cues, such as retail environments, marketing materials and interactions with service personnel. Fourthly, self-actualisation depends on 'authenticity' (or being true to oneself). There are parallels to draw here with some of the research into ethical consumption which finds some evidence that ethical consumers see themselves as belonging to a collective (for example, Shaw and Riach, 2011). Finally, the life course is seen as a series of 'passages', not fixed (as perhaps suggested by value-belief perspectives) or characterised by formal rites, but a continuous transition and trajectory of self-actualisation which involves loss and gain. Hiller and Woodall (2019), for example, discuss how the 'self' is never fully formed and dynamic, and that ethical consumption should be understood in the context of ever-shifting life goals and events which shape an individual's attitudes and behaviours.

As a focus has been placed on 'consumer identity projects' in ethical consumption research, one in which ethical consumption should be seen as one element of an individual's ongoing life project rather than process of cognitive decision-making, Garcia-Ruiz and Rodriguez-Lluesma (2014) argue for a corresponding emphasis to be placed on virtue ethics as a means to better understand an individual's *character* in moral reasoning. In doing so, it recognises that virtues (or vices) are acquired through consumption decisions and that ethical consumption research should seek to develop an understanding of an individual's search for a 'morally good life'. They argue that deontological and consequentialist moral thinking leads to a clear distinction – possibly, even, an antagonism – between ethical and non-ethical consumption. They also argue that, as a consequence, virtue ethics offers a best 'fit' with the consumer identity-work approach that is often applied in more critical perspectives on consumption. Similarly, Carrington et al. (2015) argue for a focus on the 'moral self', drawing on the concepts of life projects (ongoing consumption projects in which the self is constructed, of which there may be multiple at any one time) and life themes (broader concerns which guide the selection of desired life projects). Bartels and Reinders (2016) further explore the notion of multiple identities to understand sustainability behaviours. Caruana (2007) argues (consistent with Giddens' perspective above) for a focus on a broader conception of morality which shifts from individual motivations to one of subjective identity construction, and how ethical consumption practices can be considered from the perspective of different types of morality (for example, a more integrative individual practice of a 'care for the self' directed towards the freedom of the individual which may include intelligence, care, frugality, care or independence, and to recognise that 'being moral' is a 'work in progress'). Central to this is the recognition that what is considered to be 'right' or 'wrong' can be interpreted differently between cultures, societies and individuals, and that individuals are left to determine their own will; essentially that contemporary culture is characterised by the emancipation of the individual (Inglehart and Welzel, 2005) and consumers are faced with the consequences of their actions, but without the benefit of the guidance of traditional values, 'grand narratives' or 'regimes of truth' (Cherrier, 2007; Bauman, 1993).

Giddens (1991) further notes an aspect of identity in relation to consumption: that in capitalistic markets focused on commodification, the notion of 'lifestyle' as defined by advertisers leads to the 'project of the self' being defined by the possession of goods, which becomes in part a replacement for the genuine development of the self. There is some evidence that ethical consumers are united in feeling marginalised by this 'mainstream' consumer culture which is often focused on hyper-consumption (see, for example, Shaw and Riach, 2011). Thus, identity-related consumer research has been applied at the individual level (Luedicke et al., 2009; Cherrier, 2006), at the collective level (Bartels and Onwezen, 2014) and too, in respect of the lived world of all consumers (Cherrier and Murray, 2007; Arnould and Thompson, 2005). At the collective level, as Shaw and Riach (2011) note, ethical consumers often see themselves as part of a movement, rather than as individuals engaging isolated acts of consumption, and often this identity positions ethical consumers as being distinct from 'mainstream' consumers (Perera et al., 2018), demonstrating an 'oppositionality' at play. As a result, group solidarity is a recurrent theme in the literature, which focuses not just on the individual identities of consumers, but also social or group identities (see, for example, Bartles and Reinders, 2016) and the establishment of ethical consumption communities (for example, Papaoikonomou and Alarcón, 2017; Moraes et al., 2012), social movements (for example, Cherrier, 2007) and spaces (see, for example, Hoelscher and Chatzidakis, 2021; Chatzidakis et al., 2012).

Ethical consumption as practice

Overlapping many of the studies highlighted earlier, Szmigin and Carrigan (2006) conceptualise ethical consumption as an integrative *practice* (in which consumers see their consumption as a constituent element of their identity). As noted above, in ethical consumption research, discourse tends to focus either on the *practice of* ethical consumption or on *being* an ethical consumer. However, whilst Warde (2014) argues that the 'cultural turn' (where consumption is contextualised by webs of cultural meanings) has run its course, these are not mutually exclusive. For example, as Garcia-Ruiz and Rodriguez-Lluesma (2014) observe, virtues (exercised in the whole of an individual's 'life narratives' and as a member of communities) are sustained in practices. Indeed, Shankar et al. (2009) and Arsel and Thompson (2011) note the relationship between practice and identity; the latter being validated and reinforced by the former within the 'social world' of the consumer. Therefore, following the growing body of identity-related consumer research discussed earlier, practice theory, derived from the field of sociology, suggests a further sociological lens as a means to further understanding. Initially applied to the study of behaviour in organisations, practice theory has more recently been taken up by those with a broad interest in consumption (for example, Skålén et al., 2015; Goulding et al., 2013) and those with a special interest in *ethical* consumption and environmental behaviour change (Corsini et al., 2019; Perera et al., 2018; Moraes et al., 2017; Garcia-Ruiz and Rodriguez-Lluesma, 2014). Here, social practices are taken as the everyday and ordinary, enacted in routine and oriented (or not) towards ethical behaviour. Hargreaves (2011) suggests practice theories remove individuals from centre stage, regarding them instead as 'carriers of social practices', performing duties ascribed by the practice itself. This brings routine actions (rather than individuals) into the foreground. Moraes et al. (2012), for example, suggest we can better understand the drivers of ethical behaviour by examining the everyday habits of consumption rather than by measuring how consumers rationalise their individual inconsistencies, and Perera et al. (2018) note the benefits of understanding actual behaviour instead of intended behaviours or stated attitudes. As Moraes et al. (2012) note, many studies focusing on ethical behaviour change have been criticised for being overly focused on individual agency, and that habits and routine are a particularly significant dimension of consumer behaviour, thus finding ways to break individual or group (such as family) habits, for example, energy usage and overseas holidays, is key to increasing ethical and green consumption initiatives.

Warde (2005) defines a practice as a routinised way of behaving and understanding in different places and at different points in time, and notes that all practices require and involve consumption. Under the practice perspective, the practice itself becomes the unit of analysis, not the individuals who perform it (Hargreaves, 2011). Whilst consumption would not be considered a practice in itself under Warde's (2005) definition, as Garcia-Ruiz and Rodriguez-Lluesma (2014) argue, it may be considered as a 'domain-relative practice'. That is, it possesses its own standards of 'excellence' identifiable to other practices, and it is related to other practices to which it is subservient such as arts, science, games or sustaining family life. Studies addressing practice perspectives on consumption broadly stress its spontaneous nature and present a challenge to the received wisdom around consumer intentions. They contest the existence of a clear distinction between the objective and the subjective and argue that consumption is not induced by mechanistic and observable stimuli and neither is it based on individual conscious cognitive choices; rather, it exists inconspicuously and is embedded in practice (Hargreaves, 2011; Warde, 2005). In ethical consumption, such approaches are attractive as they contest the 'attitude behaviour choice' (ABC) models (Shove, 2010) discussed in Chapter 5 which are considered to be overly deterministic or voluntary (Huddart Kennedy et al., 2015).

One of the key thinkers in the practice theory field is the French sociologist Pierre Bourdieu, and some studies (for example, Shaw and Riach, 2011) have utilised Bourdieu's (1992) concept of 'habitus': systems of structured and structuring norms of personality constituted in individual and collective practices. Bourdieu (1992) argues that habitus is a product of history and therefore inherently tied to notions of self-identity, and that it can only be 'deduced' by relating the social conditions that generated them to the social conditions in which they are implemented. Significantly, he argues that the habitus "... is a spontaneity without consciousness or will" (p.56) which makes questions of intention 'super-fluous'. It therefore lies between the objective and the subjective; it is not produced by 'mechanical' and observable stimuli, but neither is it based on individual conscious cognitive choices; it is a form of 'inconspicuous consumption' (Hargreaves, 2011). As Warde (2005) observes, practices therefore account for both the roles of routine and emotions or desire (and thus the conative dimension of consumer behaviour recommended by Joergens (2006) for further investigation in the ethical consumer field). Bourdieu's (1984) association between habitus and the develop-ment of *taste* (as a form of cultural capital) has also been applied in understanding associations with 'ethical' movements such as the slow food movement (Lee et al., 2014). It is also important to note that in this perspective, all practices require consumption, and consumption is therefore an integral part of daily life (Warde, 2005), although there is no unilateral agreement on what defines a practice (Hargreaves, 2011). Warde (2005) argues that consumption is not a practice in itself, but a feature or part of every practice, and Connolly and Prothero (2008) argue this perspective in relation to environmental practices which are often part of wider life practices. In the context of pro-environmental behaviour change, Hargreaves (2011) notes that practices involve com-binations of images, skills and materials/technology that are integrated by practitioners using skills in repeated actions, and pro-environmental consumers will undertake various 'green consumption' practices as part of their everyday routines, and any research into ethical (or 'green') con-sumption should seek to understand these routines. Similarly, Røpke (2009) notes that this is especially important in the context of ecological consumption, where consumers are seen as skilled participants, and not 'dupes' of a market system as has perhaps been the case in other studies of consumer culture.

Typical of practice-based work is Perera et al.'s (2018) study of green consumption practices in young environmentalists, Moraes et al.'s (2017) study of ethical luxury consumption, Carrington et al.'s (2014) exploration of decision-making and daily shopping habits, Johnstone and Hooper's (2016) study of social influences on green consumption behaviour, Longo et al.'s (2017) examination of the distorting effects of consumer knowledge on sustainable decision-making and in studies of ethical clothing purchase (see, for example, Bly et al., 2015; Lundblad and Davies, 2016). This work reveals some novel perspectives on eth-ical consumption; for example, that consumers should be seen pri-marily as active participants and not passive recipients in consumption activity, engaging with producers, close friends and family, and group memberships (Perera et al., 2018), and that ethical (or non-ethical) performances are embedded within 'social performances' where objects, individual factors (such as feelings, personal experiences and cultural values) and wider cultural norms and shared values are constantly evolving and co-shared (Moraes et al., 2017). However, there is a broad conclusion derived from this work that is perhaps best represented by the title of Longo et al.'s (2017) article: *'It's not easy living a sustainable lifestyle'*.

Practice theory therefore addresses some of the problems associated with understanding the ethical consumer; it recognises that variations in behaviour are not just functions of segmentation, motivation or attitudes, and questions which benefits accrue to people within particular practices (Hargreaves, 2011; Warde, 2005). One of the key benefits of performing work that focuses qualitatively on issues of experience is that this surfaces the intricate nature of ethical consumption and the multiplicity of conflicting/conflicting agendas that apply, especially in relation to the trade-offs that consumers may often have to make to live in accordance with their values. Practice theory can also assist in focusing on the communities of practice, especially in relation to environmental socialisation in which social identities and interactions are formed (Hargreaves, 2011), and also on the virtues that are required to engage in consumption practices (Garcia-Ruiz and Rodriguez-Lluesma, 2014). Shaw and Riach (2011) also demonstrate how a 'collective habitus' of those with particular consumer identities promotes the legitimacy of ethical practices and highlight the role of research for further exploring how values and practice interact. Corsini et al. (2019) further note the possibilities for practice perspectives to better understand how sustainable consumption practices can be sustained, or indeed what keeps unsustainable modes of consumption in place. However, Røpke (2009) warns of the challenges involved in promoting sustainable consumption in the practice perspective, given that practices tend to reflect individuals' core concerns in everyday life, and these *may* conflict with environmental concerns, and Warde (2014) notes that practice theories may be insufficient on their own to capture the structural aspects of consumption at a macro level.

Sociological perspectives: summary

In contesting the notion of the ethical consumer as 'homo economicus' (that is, a 'rational maximiser' who makes conscious and deliberative choices based on a rational assessment of alternatives to maximise utility), consumer identity work and practice theories have gained significant traction in ethical consumption research in recent years. Studies adopting a sociological lens and focusing on the realm of experience have demonstrated that ethical consumption behaviour is not merely a matter of conscious decision-making, and that individuals are not necessarily autonomous and free to set their own goals and determine how to pursue them (Corsini et al., 2019). Indeed, this evidence demonstrates that there are multiple personal and situational concerns that render this a circumstantial rather than predictable pursuit, and that (ethical) consumers are not always bound by the ability to make deliberative and rational choices.

Identity work allows for the possibilities that consumers may adopt different personal identities at different times, that identities are changeable and social identities may have significance, and that (ethical) consumption should be seen as a part and consequence of an individual's ongoing 'life project'. Critics, however, may argue that adopting such a focus in ethical consumption research may place the focus on the 'self' rather than the 'other' (that is, that ethical consumption is only seen as significant to the construction of an individual's identity and not as an altruistic act focused on others), and that the 'self' risks being minimised to the consumption of goods and services rather than a more authentic search for meaning. Nevertheless, how consumers form their identities through ethical consumption remains an important dimension of our understanding about how consumers consume ethically. Practice theories are further claimed to better help understand what consumers actually do, how habits are formed and broken, and to better surface and explore the competing agendas and concerns which are likely to be at play. However, they have been acknowledged to be insufficient on their own to promote ethical consumption as individuals' core concerns may compete with ethical concerns and that a narrow focus on the individual may fail to account for the wider macro-environment in which ethical consumption takes place.

In the next chapter, we will further highlight some of the problems with the research in each of the perspectives discussed in the previous chapters and return to the question of whether the ethical consumer is, as has been claimed, a 'myth' or necessarily involves 'tragedies'. We will also explore what can be done to encourage policymakers, businesses and consumers to share responsibility to bring about positive change in relation to responsible production and consumption, before concluding by offering our views about the implications for practice and research.

6 Problems in ethical consumption research

This penultimate chapter draws on the evidence from the literature highlighted previously to directly address the problems in relation to the ethical consumption research that were noted in Chapter 2. There are clearly tensions within the field, and we will explore these tensions and debates related to awareness, knowledge and intentions, the attitude–behaviour gap, neutralisation and licensing, and emotions and outcomes (dissonance, guilt and dissatisfaction). In doing so, we will highlight some of the problems with the research in each of the previous perspectives. We will also return to the question of whether the ethical consumer is, as has been claimed, a 'myth' or necessarily involves 'tragedies', and what can be done to encourage policymakers, businesses and consumers to share responsibility to bring about positive change in relation to responsible production and consumption. Following this we will conclude by offering our views about the implications for practice and how research in the field is likely to develop in the future.

The evidence from the literature highlighted previously across the three perspectives we have identified is imbued with problems in relation to the 'ethical consumption project' in its totality, and Devinney et al. (2010) have argued that the ethical consumer is a 'myth', based on the following assertions:

- That consumers bring many values to consumption decisions
- That the context in which people behave is significant, and there is doubt as to how pervasive 'values-led' consumption is
- That individuals are bound very strongly by specific concerns which do not relate to the notion of a 'generalised' ethical consumer as portrayed in the media
- That ethical consumption behaviour is not culturally determined (and not a predominantly European pursuit, as widely believed)

DOI: 10.4324/9781003246954-6

- That the research into ethical consumption is either too general or too specific and does not address how people negotiate the complexity of the individual trade-offs of social causes.

Littler (2011) notes the other criticisms levelled at ethical consumption: that it is too large to be meaningful and often imbued with contradictions; that it cannot be progressive due to the involvement of corporates, some of whom could be accused of 'greenwashing' and that is nothing more than a high-status means of removing guilt from the 'middle classes'. There are clearly tensions within the field and the following discussion will explore these tensions and debates.

In an early study, Carrigan and Attalla (2001) questioned some of the assumptions surrounding the notion that 'good' ethical behaviour will be 'rewarded' by the market, and 'bad' behaviour 'punished' by the market. They conclude that ethics actually plays little part in consumers' decision-making; price, quality and value are the key consumer concerns, although often overlain with ethical conundrums (for example, they find that many care deeply about animal rights, but seemingly less about human rights). Likewise, Iwanow et al. (2005) found that in the clothing market specifically, ethical concerns do not significantly affect consumer choice; rather, price, quality and style are the salient factors, despite awareness of ethical issues being relatively high. Dickson (2005) also found that only a small proportion of the market (15%) would prioritise 'no sweat' principles (a guarantee that a garment was not produced in a sweatshop) over price, quality and fibre content, although she also recognises that the research measures intentions and not behaviour. She cited a number of studies which supported her findings: "For most consumers considering an apparel purchase, ethical attributes take a back seat to product features" (p.170). Other studies have continued this theme, in finding that various ethical dimensions and standards play little part in consumer decision-making (see, for example, Cailleba and Casteran, 2010). Furthermore, Valor (2008, p.315) asserts that "...consuming responsibly is seen [by consumers] as a time-consuming activity, economically disadvantageous and stressful". Indeed, as Newholm and Shaw (2007) note, there is heterogeneity and complexity in ethical consumption decisions and a body of literature has emerged which attempts to arrive at an understanding of this complexity, as follows.

Awareness, knowledge and intentions
Firstly, related in part to the segmentation perspective, there are problems around awareness and knowledge. Certainly, a number of authors have

concluded that ethical consumption is characterised by complexity in consumer choice and requires a great deal of effort and knowledge (see, for example, Hassan et al., 2013; Connolly and Shaw, 2006; Tadajewski and Wagner-Tsukamoto, 2006). Bray et al.'s (2011) research finds that an avoidance of the recipients of negative press was more prevalent than a more 'active' form of engagement, and Fisher et al. (2008) found that in the 'general' population the levels of awareness of the sustainability impacts of products (in their case, clothes) are low (across all segments), and that clothing choices are driven primarily by concerns relating to identity and economy, even with the most 'pro-environmental' segments. With regard to economy, the impact of price appears to be driven by the age (or 'life stage') of consumers; for example, young people in particular purchase clothing from low-budget retailers, well aware that it will not be durable (Cooper et al., 2016). Even where consumers possess a significant knowledge, there exist dilemmas about making the 'right' choice in consumption decisions (Connolly and Prothero, 2008). Following from Shiu et al. (2011) who find three dimensions to uncertainty (knowledge, choice and evaluation), Hassan et al. (2013) highlight the importance of the concept of uncertainty in explaining why ethical consumers may not act in accordance with their values and develop a conceptual model to explain its role. They find that uncertainty can be classified in three ways: in knowledge (as above), choice (when information on which to base comparative judgements is scarce) and evaluation (how ethical information can be made sense of in the light of other known information about products and retailers). Antecedents relate to complexity as above, but also ambiguity, conflicts and credibility, with the outcomes being a delayed purchase, compromised beliefs or negative emotions. This raises the question of how consumers might process and act on such complexity and consumer confusion from the complexity in choice may support the need for clearer consumer guidelines. Indeed, Devinney et al. (2010) argue consumers who factor in the social impacts of their purchases do so very specifically and ethical choices rarely bear any relation to accepted definitions of 'ethical consumption'.

Valor (2007) contends that consumers adopt these strategies in order to deal with complexity in choice, which specifically occurs when the sheer number of potential ethical issues leads individuals to champion a select number of causes. As previously discussed, Shaw et al. (2000) suggest that the two key factors which drive this 'bounded rationality' are ethical obligation and self-identity. However, Tadajewski and Wagner-Tsukamoto (2006) observe that where awareness and knowledge is high, consumers are particularly ineffective shoppers due to 'paralysis' and that "...green consumer

behaviour [is] dependent, to some degree, on a veil of ignorance...
Here, then, is the tragedy of the green consumer" (p.18). Similarly,
Carrigan and Attalla (2001) observe that making consistent ethical
judgements that avoid harming all stakeholders can be extremely difficult. Conversely, Valor (2007) proposes that the higher the visibility
of ethical problems, the more likely ethical purchasing will occur.
Nevertheless, there is conflicting evidence that such problems affect
buyer behaviour in a significant way on the high street. A similar
issue with different outcomes is highlighted by Shaw et al. (2006)
who discover problems for 'highly motivated ethical consumers' who
lack the necessary information to make educated decisions. Purchase
decisions here are referred to as "a gamble ... guesswork ... [or] ...
hope" (p.437). As Hiller Connell (2010) finds, these problems can be
even more complex in clothing purchase, where sometimes specialist
knowledge of fibres and manufacturing processes, for example,
may be sought. Following Carrigan and Attalla's (2001) model
characterising consumers by intention and awareness, these problems
related to awareness and motivation can therefore be represented in
the matrix shown in Figure 1.

The boxes in the top half of the matrix display the outcomes proposed
by Hassan et al. (2013) and Tadajewski and Wagner-Tsukamoto (2006)
(high awareness/knowledge and high motivation), Hiller Connell (2010)
and Shaw et al. (2006) (high motivation/low knowledge). Consumers
with low awareness, knowledge or motivation will clearly not take ethical issues into account (as demonstrated by Fisher et al., 2008). There

Knowledge

		High	*Low*
Motivation	High	*The paralysed consumer* Hassan et al. (2013) Tadajewski and Wagner-Tsukamoto (2006)	*The gambler* Hiller Connell (2010) Shaw et al. (2006) Carrigan and Attalla (2001)
	Low	*The unconcerned consumer*	*The unaware consumer* Fisher et al. (2008) Valor (2007)

Figure 1 Consumer motivation towards ethical issues vs. knowledge of ethical
practices

is little research regarding consumers in the bottom-left hand box of the quadrant; however, it may be assumed that if knowledge is high, but motivation is low, these consumers have made a conscious choice not to buy ethically. Areas of research interest are clearly focused on the consumers for whom awareness or motivation is high or raising consumer awareness. In all four cases, 'successful' ethical consumption appears to be unlikely, reinforcing the nature of the 'tragedy' in ethical consumption.

Tadajewski and Wagner-Tsukamoto (2006) and Wagner (2003) further argue that research into 'green' consumer behaviour which does not place consumers in context (as outlined in Chapter 5) is flawed, and by doing so through an anthropological approach conclude that, as previously explored, there are significant differences between intention to purchase, awareness and actual purchase behaviour. Similarly, Devinney et al. (2010) argue that context is 'overwhelming' in determining behaviour, and examinations of segmentation variables or intentions which do not account for context are substantially flawed. Indeed, Shaw and Clarke (1999) conclude that the links between thought and action are extremely complex, and this tension, or gap, between attitudes and behaviour is a well-recognised phenomenon, and which has been the subject of much discussion. Furthermore, this is a multidisciplinary discussion which has been explored well beyond the fields of business, management and economics, with aspects of ethical consumption being investigated in literature from the arts and humanities, psychology and social sciences (Carrington et al., 2021).

The attitude–behaviour gap

Since early studies such as Carrigan and Attalla (2001), who highlighted the conflicts and tensions between attitudes and behaviour, a significant amount of recent research has focused on the 'attitude–behaviour gap'. Carrigan and Attalla (2001) argued that possessing the motivation, knowledge *and ability* to make effective consumer decisions is not sufficient; the motivation and knowledge must be acted upon. Consequently, various studies have examined what Newholm (2005, p.108) refers to as the "irresolvable debates ... around the attitude behaviour gap", which find that consumers possess socially responsible attitudes, but these attitudes are rarely acted upon (see, for example, Govind et al., 2019; Carrington et al., 2015; Hassan et al., 2016; Johnstone and Tan, 2015). Whilst Dickson (2005, p.170) refers to other "...unforeseen conditions" which could affect purchase behaviour, a number of explanatory factors for the gap are proposed.

The first factor relates to complexity in consumer choice. As Schwartz (2010) recognises, evaluating claims of consumer obligation are often inherently problematic as the moral issues invoked are frequently complex and not typical to 'everyday life'; for example, supply chains and manufacturing processes are often extremely sophisticated, involving many tiers of suppliers and 'hidden' processes. Gummerus et al. (2017) propose that consumers perceive fewer benefits when that ethical consumption is driven by limitations in choice and that ethical consumption can be positively enhanced by participation in online communities. Clouder and Harrison (2005) suggest that the array of factors involved in making purchase decisions rarely allow large numbers of consumers to switch to more 'ethical' options, although there are examples of this occurring in 'mature' ethical markets (free-range eggs, for example) and a wider range of ethically orientated products have become available in many markets since their study was conducted. Claudy et al. (2013) find that in facing this complexity, consumers take 'cognitive short cuts', and will simplify decisions by finding rationalisation for 'easier' alternative behaviours. Valor (2007, p.689) suggests that the gap can be explained by "...the complexity of human cognition and the trade-offs that consumers have to make in order to live up to their values". She concludes that 'ambivalence' is the theme which characterises consumer feelings and actions in (clothing) purchase; that is, that there exist trade-offs and tensions between what consumers feel they ought to do, what they want to do, and what they are able to do. The concept of the trade-off will be revisited in subsequent analysis, although feelings of powerlessness can also be significant (Johnstone and Tan, 2015), including feelings of distance; that is, that it is not felt by consumers that ethical issues in clothing affect them directly (Hassan et al., 2013; Joergens, 2006). Govind et al. (2019) posit that consumers' implicit attitudes, which may remain relatively unaffected by stimuli, play a stronger role than explicit attitudes in consumers' behaviour and preferences in ethical purchase decisions, offering an explanation for the attitude–behaviour gap and thus creating difficulties for businesses in understanding and anticipating consumers' buying patterns. The second is *ease*, including barriers such as time, price, a lack of available products and perceived effort (Johnstone and Tan, 2015; Valor, 2008). Linked to this are notions of practice; Bray et al. (2011) highlight the role of inertia as a key barrier to behaviour change, and as Moraes et al. (2012) note, consumer action is characterised by habitual behaviour, and they argue that the attitude–behaviour gap can be reduced through the formation of 'new consumption communities' which promote 'collective choice editing', or Carrington et al. (2010) recommend in-store reminders to help consumers 'snap out' of their usual habits. Thirdly, reasons which might be best labelled as cynicism appear to be significant. This includes doubts about the 'ethicality' of ethical alternatives (Johnstone and Tan, 2015) or the claims made by organisations (Bray et al., 2011). Joergens (2006) also finds an unwillingness to 'judge' the ethical standards of overseas companies; Johnstone and Tan (2015) discover evidence that there is a 'stigma' associated with being 'green' that can conflict with perceptions of self-identity.

Neutralisation and licensing

A further challenge for ethical consumption lies in what Chatzidakis et al. (2004, 2006) define as 'neutralisation', a means for coping with cognitive dissonance following 'attitude–behaviour discrepancy' in ethical consumption (where the attitude–behaviour discrepancy might be considered to be a 'violation of personal ethical beliefs and values'). The five neutralisation techniques in the consumption context stated are as follows:

- Denial of responsibility (where individuals do not consider themselves personally accountable because factors beyond one's control were operating)
- Denial of injury (where misconduct is not considered serious because no party directly suffers as a result)
- Denial of victim (where the blame for personal actions is countered because the violated party is considered to be to blame)
- Condemning the condemners (where individuals deflect accusations of misconduct due to accusations that the violated parties act, or would act, in the same way)
- Appeal to higher loyalties (where one argues that norm-violating behaviour is the result of an attempt to actualise a higher-order value).

Chatzidakis et al. (2004) propose that such neutralisation techniques might occur at any stage of the ethical decision-making process. However, although they note that neutralisation may normally be viewed as occurring post-purchase, they also claim that it can occur pre-purchase to make 'unethical' behaviour possible. Indeed, the focus of neutralisation theory here is to understand how consumers may mitigate the impact of their ethically questionable activities. The notion of mitigation is also developed by Mazar and Zhong (2009), who argue that purchasing 'green' products can act as a 'licence' to engage in sub-sequent unethical behaviour. That is, that virtuous behaviour is often undertaken as a response to moral 'transgressions', and by the same token once a good deed (such as an ethical purchase) has been under-taken, the moral implications of a subsequent act are less likely to be considered. Here, Mazar and Zhong (2009) link the fields of consumer ethics and ethical consumption to imply that ethical consumption may 'license' consumers to engage in dishonest or other unethical consump-tion behaviours. Monbiot (2009) suggests that this principle can be seen in action with consumers who engage in small 'green' acts (such as recycling) to justify much worse 'non-green' behaviour (such as taking numerous long-haul flights).

Emotions and outcomes: dissonance, guilt and dissatisfaction

As noted earlier, Hassan et al. (2013) provide a reminder that, for eth-ical consumers at least, there are negative emotional outcomes such as frustration or helplessness which may result from engaging in behaviour that compromises ethical beliefs or values. Gregory-Smith et al. (2013) suggest that the role of emotions could be one explanatory factor in the existence of the attitude–behaviour gap, as emotions may override attitudes in decision-making. Whilst they find a hedonic aspect to posi-tive purchasing, they also discover that guilt is the most salient nega-tive emotion associated with dissonant behaviour, along with regret, disappointment and embarrassment, although they find that (as with licensing behaviour) guilt can be compensated with previously 'good' behaviour. Other studies have also examined the role of emotions in ethical consumer behaviour. For example, Acuti et al. (2022) provide a review of the literature on unintended negative side effects of product and service sustainability on consumer behaviour. They identify three main 'cognitive mechanisms' (information elaboration, product percep-tion bias and self-perception), and several 'emotionally aversive states' (such as anxiety, shame, guilt or regret). Chatzidakis (2015) draws on psychoanalytic theory to consider guilt in ethical consumer choices. Whilst the focus is perhaps on consumer ethics, he notes that it is neces-sary to move away from cognitive and rational perspectives and that the market itself can create guilt that can be alleviated through consuming 'ethical' products and services. Conversely, Bray et al. (2011) also find that consumers may develop a sense of guilt retrospectively following a choice not to buy an ethical option (although they find it is not part of the decision-making process, and a post-purchase response). Antonetti and Maklan (2015), however, find that the role of guilt is more cyclical;

they argue that the regulation of consumers' behaviour is mediated by perceived consumer effectiveness, and that this is reinforced as consumer agency when feelings of guilt are experienced post-purchase, thus moderating future behaviour. Chen and Moosmayer (2018) emphasise that the impact of guilt appeals when promoting ethical products can depend on the culture, religion or belief system of the target consumers. As previously argued in relation to the context-specific nature of consumption, Gregory-Smith et al. (2013) argue that the role of emotions alongside other contextual factors in explaining the attitude–behaviour gap renders it transitory.

From tragedies and myths to trade-offs

Each of the areas of consumer research into ethical consumption carries both benefits and problems. However, they are not necessarily mutually exclusive, and should not be seen in isolation. These studies do, however, begin to highlight some of the complexities and contradictions in the field; Connolly and Shaw (2006) conclude that there is a great deal of diversity in consumer views and behaviour and that organisations rarely understand these opinions. This is further complicated by the complex relationships between awareness, attitudes and behaviour, the problems in adopting a purely psychological or sociological perspective and the methods used to research consumer ethics. Of course, the consequences are that if ethical consumption is complex for those with ethical awareness and intentions, this will be more the case for those without such motivations.

As the previous discussion has shown, many studies have tended to overstate the importance of segmentation variables which are inherently unstable or rational, and cognitive decision-making which is also limited and limiting in explaining the complex and contextually based domain of ethical consumption. It should also be noted that, with a limited number of exceptions (for example, Hiller and Woodall, 2019; Antonetti and Maklan, 2015), few studies have attempted to understand the effect of ethical consumer behaviour on the post-purchase evaluation of purchase and on intention to (re)purchase. This is significant in terms of sustaining practices as previously discussed, and also from a commercial imperative because there is significant evidence to suggest that there is a positive connection between positive post-purchase evaluations and profitability, and a negative correlation between negative post-purchase evaluations and profitability. Kincaid et al. (1998) note that in the clothing industry such post-purchase evaluations are important in relation to organisational performance, and a number of authors have since proposed a positive relationship between CSR and business performance, perhaps at least partly explained through a link with satisfaction (Luo and Bhattacharya, 2006; Capaldi, 2005; Balabanis et al., 1998).

Expectancy-value models under the psychological perspective have been argued to reduce ethical decision-making to a purely cognitive process of arriving at utilitarian outcomes which predominantly serve self-interested behaviours; to be deficient in explaining ethical or moral motivations; are poor predictors of likely behaviour and assume consumers have full control (de Groot et al., 2016). In rejecting consumers as rational individual-optimisers, Thøgersen (1996) argues the case for moral norm theory, which focuses on values and which marketers should attempt to 'awaken' in promoting pro-environmental behaviour (de Groot et al., 2016). Indeed, as Devinney et al. (2010) argue, values *are* brought into the purchasing context, but there are many other contributors to the consumption decision. The sociological perspective in terms of self- and social-identities appears to address many of the problems associated with marketing and philosophical perspectives, although as with expectancy-value models perhaps runs the risk that the notion of responsible choices relates only to self-fulfilment. Likewise, practice theory appears to be helpful in further understanding consumption contexts, which may result in conflicts between individuals' core concerns in everyday life and environmental concerns, although as noted previously may be insufficient on their own to understand ethical consumption outside of an individual's 'life world'.

As argued in Hiller and Woodall (2019), whilst each of these approaches and perspectives has its own attractions and pitfalls, a concept that emerges as a central theme and unites these four areas of literature is that of *trade-offs*. As Arnould and Thompson (2005, p.871) state, "Consumer identity projects are typically considered to be goal-driven, although the aims pursued may be ... marked by points of conflict, internal contradictions, ambivalence and even pathology". A number of the studies discussed in this book also highlight their importance, as well as the notions of conflict, contradictions, compromise and ambivalence. A more formal notion of trade-offs as discrete decision-making processes is also found significant in emerging evidence on ethical consumption (see, for example, Perera et al., 2018; Ha-Brookshire and Norum, 2011). Such studies have sought to foreground trade-offs, exploring these via distinct case-specific scenarios that focus explicitly on competing options. Devinney et al. (2010), for example, apply a 'best–worst' experiment in which consumers are asked to rate the relative importance of objects of conflicting perceptual difference and the trade-off. Glac (2009) similarly considers trade-offs involving different types of functional consequence (the results of investing in two different pension schemes), whilst Luchs and Kumar (2017) appraise contrasting merits of both aesthetic versus sustainable product attributes and utilitarian versus sustainable product attributes. As an alternative to best–worst comparisons, others suggest cost–benefit as pertinent competing options. These focus often on how price influences consumers where virtuous options are marked higher than the competition (Lim et al., 2014; Abrantes Ferreira et al., 2010; De Pelsmacker et al., 2005).

The literature pertaining to trade-offs construes these frequently as conflicts that apply at a cognitive level of decision-making. Hassan et al. (2013) and Schröder and McEachern (2004), for example, describe contradictions that arise from guilt and the breaking of ethical rules; McGoldrick and Freestone (2008) argue that we accrue a 'balance sheet' of gains and losses that are in opposition, and state consequently this represents a conflict to be resolved. Such conflicts have been described as representing 'difficult value judgements' (Moisander, 2007) or 'hard choices' (McShane et al., 2011), whilst both Johnstone and Tan (2015) and Valor (2007) and refer to compromises or sacrifices made. The role of rational agency in settling internal disputes is evident in these accounts, and all trade-offs invoked imply the consumer is engaged in an act of preferential judgement.

In the psychological perspective, expectancy-value models rely on rational utilitarian trade-offs (de Groot et al., 2016), and in the moral norm perspective Jägel et al. (2012, p.396) conclude that "consumers have to compromise and balance their conflicting end goals", thus supporting the emerging body of evidence for the existence of trade-offs. In practice perspectives, Perera et al. (2018) find that young environmentalists have to make critical trade-offs to be environmentally conscious, and Røpke (2009) notes conflicts between individuals' core concerns in everyday life, and environmental concerns. Similarly, Littler (2011) argues that ethical consumption is increasingly becoming what might best be describes as 'contradictory consumption' as it often involves a number of different practices which are often in conflict with one another (buying locally grown vegetables but Fair Trade wine from Chile rather than something locally produced, for example). Further, in linking identity and practice approaches, Shaw and Riach (2011) note that the practice of ethical consumption and the identity of 'ethical consumer' may be characterised by contradictions, which carries a need to understand the tensions created when values and actions may mismatch. Finally, as Devinney et al. (2010) argue, behaviour (and especially ethical consumer behaviour, which involves difficult and inconvenient choices) is based upon trade-offs of valuation, and they argue that research should examine the inconsistencies between attitudes and behaviour and consumer choices.

7 Conclusion

Observations on state of the art

As we have shown, the research and evidence to date related to ethical consumption has grown from a 'niche' preoccupation to a mainstream and significant (and growing) consumer and business issue covering a variety of sectors, and ethical consumption research correspondingly has grown in its breadth and depth. However, we would argue that studies of ethical consumption have sought to understand more and more about increasing areas of narrow focus. As the previous chapters have demonstrated, many of these approaches have their limitations or have resulted in claimed problems with the 'ethical consumption project'. Perhaps unfairly these problems place some blame on consumers for failing to live in accordance with their stated values, characterised particularly by the 'attitude–behaviour gap'. The reality is perhaps despite research increasingly demonstrating that ethics is a significant and growing concern to consumers, albeit characterised by some scepticism when organisations fail to engender trust amongst their stakeholders, little is known about the totality of factors which influence consumer decision-making.

We have explored ethical consumption from discrete perspectives which we believe to be the dominant perspectives in ethical consumer research, as presented in the business and marketing literature, mindful however that it is increasingly becoming characterised by interdisciplinary approaches (Carrington et al., 2021) and that, significantly it is likely that this occurs across multiple consumer groups and product/service categories, involving cognitive, emotional and behavioural dimensions of consumer behaviour. Each of the perspectives we have explored carries its own benefits and drawbacks, but pejorative themes of anxiety, dispute, sacrifice and conflict persist in much of the research. However, despite various claims about the 'attitude–behaviour gap', we contend that consumers have increasingly higher expectations of company practices, seeking to be the best that they can be, and organisations

DOI: 10.4324/9781003246954-7

need to respond accordingly. Indeed, ethical consumption extends to myriad practices which are integrated into an individual's search for a morally good life; as Bauman (1993) argues, humans are not inherently good or evil, but are ambivalent (as suggested in the ethical consumption domain). This leaves little room for a 'logically coherent ethical code' which guarantees ethical conduct, but recognising the power of individual and moral conscience means that consumer responses to the moral obligations they face are varied. As Wiggins (2006) notes, morality cannot be separated from the 'everyday meaning of everyday life' and we would encourage researchers and practitioners to adopt a 'human-centred' approach which accounts for non-binary perspectives and places the individual centre-stage as both a rational and emotional being who engages in a number of learned patterns of habits and preferences.

We therefore recommend that research into ethical consumption recognises ethical pluralism, which holds that several moral standards may be relevant depending on the specific situation; sometimes these moral standards will produce the same result, sometimes they will conflict (Hinman, 2003), and which seeks to understand ethical consumption in the totality of an individual's life and practices. That is, studies often treat ethical consumption as an all-encompassing practice which applies across multiple purchases or behaviours. For example, it might be assumed (either explicitly or implicitly) that a predisposition towards Fair Trade will be enacted across other similarly focused product categories (Ma et al., 2012; White et al., 2012). This suggests voluntary simplifiers will adopt complementary practices across all of their consumption activities (Cherrier, 2007), or green consumers will behave consistently across all categories (Lu et al., 2015; Connolly and Prothero, 2008). However, further research might seek to explore the extent to which assumed integrative or holistic approaches actually exist. In terms of recommendations for future research, we see opportunities for more trans-disciplinary perspectives (Carrington et al., 2021) which move away from a narrow focus on buying motivations to exploring the role of ethics in the totality of consumers' lives, and also at a macro-level in terms of the cultural and socio-economic contexts in which consumption occurs.

Further, with regard to the research into ethical consumer behaviour we have presented, we note the following salient points: firstly, regardless of stated problems with expectancy-value models, ethical obligation and self-identity are key constructs which also recur throughout the literature and which may be characterised by the priorities held by individuals in relation to their values. Despite Devinney et al.'s (2010) warning against a focus on values, they remain an important dimension of ethical consumer behaviour (Jägel et al., 2012), and Hiller and Woodall (2019) and Shaw and Riach (2011) highlight the need for research to further explore how values and practice interact. Certainly, the importance of context, practices and consumer identities remain pressing factors; purely cognitive (rational), affective (emotional) or conative (behavioural) studies which aim to understand how consumers deal with making trade-offs are likely to provide an incomplete picture of the complex practices and decisions which face individuals. We encourage you to consider that 'ethical consumption' is not a truth or objective in itself which has to be 'achieved'; we would advocate the recognition of the multiplicity of moral standards and inconsistent attitudes and behaviours that are brought into consumption and view these as part of a unification and continuous merging that occurs throughout the flow of individual experience (Hiller and Woodall, 2019). As Rorty (1995) observes, an individual's notions of right or good change depending on previous experiences of success or failure in doing right and good. Consequently, we challenge assertions that ethical consumption should be characterised by its 'failures' or 'contradictions'. However, nor do we view ethical consumers as mythical; they are, rather, an entity that exists but is never fully formed, as consumers strive to be the best they can be. By giving emphasis to both functional consequences (occurrences) and psycho-social consequences (feelings), research should acknowledge the potential for *being* as well as *doing* in an ethical context. These 'middle ground' perspectives which identify the integrated nature of trade-offs and values in consumption practice have become increasingly popular in ethical consumption research (see, for example, Hiller and Woodall, 2019, and Lundblad and Davies, 2016).

There is clearly also an ongoing need to continue to educate consumers and managers about the impacts of their practices in response to frequent and dynamic changes in various aspects of ethics. In terms of policy and education therefore, as with the focus in the ethical consumption literature, research into sustainability education is often characterised by a 'theory–practice gap' and often treats the learner as a rational, cognitively bound decision-maker (Painter et al., 2019). However, as Allen et al. (2019) argue, critically reflexive approaches are required to bring about shifts in learning; these may include strategies such as experiential learning (Shephard, 2008), reflexive practice (Dianati and Banfield, 2020; Millar and Price, 2018), emotional awareness (Wilson, 2007), systems thinking (Earle and Leyva-de la Hiz, 2020; Painter-Morland et al., 2016), democratic pedagogy (Tarrant and Thiele, 2016) and transdisciplinary practices (Baumber, 2022), and we would encourage policymakers and educators to consider these approaches. Further, Carbon Literacy Training is one of many potentially effective methods of imparting such information, by teaching educators and organisations how to enhance the level of sustainability in their work and as consumers, with the opportunity to disseminate their knowledge and practice to influence colleagues, friends and family. Furthermore, Painter-Morland et al. (2016) advocate moving beyond teaching ethical content to consider how universities themselves can become holistically sustainable.

Finally, there is a need for companies to improve their own ethical practices and to support consumers to make more ethical choices through communication, education and action. Recognising, as explored in Chapter 5, that consumption occurs often through highly routinised behaviour and sometimes at an unconscious level, assisting consumers to change habits must be a cornerstone of any organisation's strategy. We encourage practitioners to explore how their consumers' habits are formed and broken, and also to help those who wish to consume ethically through the provision of clear information and education. In marketing research, this means to better understand the practices that underpin behaviour change through the formation or breaking of habits. That is, that ethically focused behaviour can be better understood by recognising consumers' habits holistically, characterised by shifting life-centred priorities. In terms of marketing communications, we encourage moving away from simplistic promotional messages which seek to appeal to a constrained consumer identity or incomplete range of emotions. Instead, we advocate the use of open and transparent marketing campaigns, which engage customers as partners, seeing ethical consumption as a shared responsibility in which both organisations and consumers engage in a mutual and continuous process of learning and improvement.

References

Abrantes Ferreira, D., Gonçalves Avila, M., & Dias de Faria, M. (2010). Corporate social responsibility and consumers' perception of price. *Social Responsibility Journal*, *6*(2), 208–221.

Accenture (2020). *How Covid-19 Will Permanently Change Consumer Behaviour* [online]. Available at: www.accenture.com/_acnmedia/PDF-134/Accenture-COVID19-Consumer-Behaviour-Survey-Research-PoV.pdf#zoom=40

Acuti, D., Pizzetti, M., & Dolnicar, S. (2022). When sustainability backfires: A review on the unintended negative side-effects of product and service sustainability on consumer behavior. *Psychology and Marketing*. DOI: 10.1002/mar.21709

Aertsens, J., Verbeke, W., Mondelaers, K., & Van Huylenbroeck, G. (2009). Personal determinants of organic food consumption: A review. *British Food Journal*, *111*(10), 1140–1167.

Ajzen, I. (1991). *Attitudes, Personality and Behavior*. Milton Keynes: Open University Press.

Agag, G., & Colmekcioglu, N. (2020). Understanding guests' behavior to visit green hotels: The role of ethical ideology and religiosity. *International Journal of Hospitality Management*, *91* (October), 102679.

Allen, S., Cunliffe, A.L., & Easterby-Smith, M. (2019). Understanding sustainability through the lens of ecocentric radical-reflexivity: Implications for management education. *Journal of Business Ethics*. https://doi.org/10.1007/s10551-016-3420-3

Alsaad, A., Saif-Alyousfi, A.Y., & Elrehail, H. (2020). Religiosity, idealism, and ethical consumption: the mediating effect of perceived customer effectiveness and moral obligation. *Journal of Social Marketing*, *11*(1), 25–43.

Anderson, W.T. & Cunningham W.H. (1972). The socially conscious consumer. *Journal of Marketing*, *36* (July), 23–31.

Antonetti, P., & Maklan, S. (2015). Feelings that make a difference: How guilt and pride convince consumers of the effectiveness of sustainable consumption choices. *Journal of Business Ethics*, *124*, 117–134.

Arli, D., & Pekerti, A. (2017). Who is more ethical? Cross-cultural comparison of consumer ethics between religious and non-religious consumers. *Journal of Consumer Behaviour*, *16*(1), 82–98.

Arnould, E.J., & Thompson, C.J. (2005). Consumer culture theory (CCT): Twenty years of research. *Journal of Consumer Research, 31*(4), 868–882.

Arsel, Z., & Thompson, C.J. (2011). Demythologising consumption practices: how consumers protect their field-dependent identity investments from devaluing marketplace myths. *Journal of Consumer Research, 37*(Februray), 791–806.

Auger, P., Burke, P., Devinney, T.M., & Louviere, J.J. (2003). What will consumers pay for social product features? *Journal of Business Ethics, 42*(3), 381–304.

Auger, P., & Devinney, T.M. (2007). Do what consumers say matter? The misalignment of preferences with unconstrained ethical intentions. *Journal of Business Ethics, 76*, 361–383.

Babakus, E., Cornwell, T.B., Mitchell, V.M., & Schlegelmilch, B. (2004). Reactions to unethical consumer behavior across six countries. *Journal of Consumer Marketing, 21*(4), 254–263.

Balabanis, G., Phillips, H.C., & Lyall, J. (1998). Corporate social responsibility and economic performance in the top British companies: Are they linked? *European Business Review, 98*(1), 25–44.

Balderjahn, I., Buerke, A., Kirchgeorg, M., Peyer, M., Seegebarth, B., & Wiedmann, K.P. (2013). Consciousness for sustainable consumption: Scale development and new insights in the economic dimension of consumers' sustainability. *AMS Review, 3*(4), 181–192.

Bartels, J., & Onwezen, M.C. (2014). Consumers' willingness to buy products with environmental and ethical claims: the roles of social representations and social identity. *International Journal of Consumer Studies, 38*, 82–89.

Bartels, J., & Reinders, M.J. (2016). Consuming apart, together: The role of multiple identities in sustainability behaviour. *International Journal of Consumer Studies, 40*(4), 444–452.

Bauman, Z. (1993). *Postmodern Ethics*. Oxford: Blackwell.

Bauman, Z. (2008). *Does Ethics Have a Chance in a World of Consumers?* Cambridge, MA: Harvard University Press.

Baumber, A. (2022). Transforming sustainability education through transdisciplinary practice. *Environment, Development and Sustainability, 24*, 7622–7639.

Birch, S. (2007). Ethical Trade Initiative: toothless talking shop? *Ethical Consumer, 104*, 38.

Bourdieu, P. (1992). *The Logic of Practice*. Cambridge: Polity Press.

Belk, R.W. (1988). Possessions and the extended self. *Journal of Consumer Research, 15*(2), 139–168.

Bloemer, J., & Dekker, D. (2007). Effects of personal values on customer satisfaction: An empirical test of the value percept disparity model and the value disconfirmation model. *International Journal of Bank Marketing, 25*(5), 276 291.

Bly, S., Gwozdz, W., & Reisch, L.A. (2015). Exit from the high street. An exploratory study of sustainable fashion consumption pioneers. *International Journal of Consumer Studies, 39*(2), 125–135.

Bourdieu, P. (1984). *Distinction.* London: Routledge.

Bourdieu, P. (1992). *The Logic of Practice.* Cambridge: Polity Press.

Bray, J., Johns, N., & Kilburn, D. (2011). An exploratory study into the factors impeding ethical consumption. *Journal of Business Ethics, 98,* 597–608.

Brinkmann, J. (2004). Looking at consumer behaviour in a moral perspective. *Journal of Business Ethics, 51,* 129–141.

Brown, S. (2006). Recycling postmodern marketing. *The Marketing Review, 6,* 211–230.

Burke, P.F., Eckert, C., & Davis, S. (2014). Segmenting consumers' reasons for and against ethical consumption. *European Journal of Marketing, 48*(11/12), 2237–2261.

Cailleba, P., & Casteran H. (2010). Do ethical values work? A quantitative study of the impact of fair trade coffee on consumer behaviour. *Journal of Business Ethics, 97,* 613–624.

Capaldi, N. (2005). Corporate social responsibility and the bottom line. *International Journal of Social Economics, 32*(5), 408–423.

Carrigan, M., & Attalla, A. (2001). The myth of the ethical consumer; do ethics matter in purchase behaviour? *Journal of Consumer Marketing, 18*(7), 560–577.

Carrigan, M., & de Pelsmacker, P. (2009). Will ethical consumers sustain their values in the global credit crunch? *International Marketing Review, 26*(6), 674–687.

Carrigan, M., Szmigin, I., & Wright, J. (2004). Shopping for a better world? An interpretive study of the potential for ethical consumption within the older market. *Journal of Consumer Marketing, 21*(6), 401–417.

Carrington, M.J, Chatzidakis, A., Goworek, H., & Shaw, D. (2021). Consumption ethics: A review and analysis of future directions for interdisciplinary research. *Journal of Business Ethics, 168,* 215–238.

Carrington, M.J., Neville, B.A., & Canniford, R. (2015). Unmanageable multiplicity: Consumer transformation towards moral self coherence. *European Journal of Marketing, 49*(7/8), 1300–1325.

Carrington, M.J., Neville, B.A., & Whitwell, G.J. (2010). Why ethical consumers don't walk the talk: Towards a framework for understanding the gap between ethical purchase intentions and actual buying behavior of ethically minded consumers. *Journal of Business Ethics, 97,* 139–158.

Carrington, M.J., Neville, B.A., & Whitwell, G.J. (2014). Lost in translation: Exploring the ethical consumer intention–behavior gap. *Journal of Business Research, 67*(1), 2759–2767.

Carrington, M.J., Zwick, D., & Neville, B. (2016). The ideology of the ethical consumption gap. *Marketing Theory, 16*(1), 21–38.

Carroll, A.B. (1991). The pyramid of corporate social responsibility: Toward the moral management of organisational stakeholders. *Business Horizons,* July/August, 39–48.

Caruana, R. (2007). A sociological perspective of consumption morality. *Journal of Consumer Behaviour, 6*(Sep–Oct), 287–304.

Castaldo, S., Perrini, F., Misani, N., & Tencati, A. (2009). The missing link between corporate social responsibility and consumer trust: The case of fair trade products. *Journal of Business Ethics, 84*, 1–15.

Chandler, J.D., & Vargo, S.L. (2011). Contextualization and value-in-context: How context frames exchange. *Marketing Theory, 11*(1), 35–49.

Chatzidakis, A. (2015). Guilt and ethical choice in consumption: A psychoanalytic perspective. *Marketing Theory, 15*(1), 79–93.

Chatzidakis, A., Hibbert, S., Mittusis, D., & Smith, A. (2004). Virtue in consumption? *Journal of Marketing Management, 20*, 527–544.

Chatzidakis, A., Hibbert, S., & Smith, A. (2006). Ethically concerned, yet unethically behaved: towards an updated understanding of consumer's (un)ethical decision making. *Advances in Consumer Research, 33*, 693–698.

Chatzidakis, A., Maclaran, P., & Bradshaw, A. (2012). Heterotopian space and the utopics of ethical and green consumption. *Journal of Marketing Management, 28*(3–4), 494–515.

Chen, Y., & Moosmayer, D. (2018). When guilt is not enough: Interdependent self-construal as moderator of the relationship between guilt and ethical consumption in a Confucian context. *Journal of Business Ethics, 161*(1), 551–572.

Cherrier, H. (2007). Ethical consumption practices: Co-production of self-expression and social recognition. *Journal of Consumer Behaviour, 6*(Sept/Oct), 321–335.

Cherrier, H. (2006). Consumer identity and moral obligations in non-plastic bag consumption: A dialectical perspective. *International Journal of Consumer Studies, 30*(5), 515–523.

Cherrier, H., & Murray, J. (2007). Reflexive dispossession and the self: Constructing a processual theory of identity. *Consumption, Markets and Culture, 10*(1), 1–29.

Chowdhury, R.M.M.I. (2020). Personal values and consumers' ethical beliefs: The mediating roles of moral identity and Machiavellianism. *Journal of Macromarketing, 40*(3), 415–431.

Claudy, M.C., Peterson, M., & O'Driscoll, A. (2013). Understanding the attitude–behaviour gap for renewable energy systems using behavioural reasoning theory. *Journal of Macromarketing, 33*(4), 273–287.

Clean Clothes Campaign. (2013). *Still Waiting Report.* Clean Clothes Campaign and International Labor Rights Forum [online]. Available at: https://cleanclothes.org/file-repository/resources-publications-still-waiting/view

Clouder, S., & Harrison, R. (2005). 'The Effectiveness of Ethical Consumer Behaviour'. *In:* R. Harrison, T. Newholm and D. Shaw (eds.). *The Ethical Consumer.* London: Sage Publications.

Cohen, J.B., Fishbein, M., & Ahtola, O.T. (1972). The nature and uses of expectancy-value models in consumer attitude research. *Journal of Marketing Research, 9*(4), 456–460.

Connolly, J., & Prothero, A. (2008). Sustainable consumption: Consumption, consumers and the commodity discourse. *Consumption, Markets and Culture*, 6(4), 275–291.

Connolly, J., & Shaw, D. (2006). Identifying fair trade in consumption choice. *Journal of Strategic Marketing*, 14 (Dec), 353–368.

Cooper, T., Oxborrow, L., Claxton, S., Goworek, H., Hill, H., & McLaren, A. (2016). *Strategies to improve design and testing for clothing longevity*. Report for DEFRA. 1248715_Cooper.pdf (ntu.ac.uk). www.ntu.ac.uk/__data/ass ets/pdf_file/0039/906897/strategies-improve-design-testing-clothing-longev ity.pdf

Corsini, F., Laurenti, R., Meinherz, F., Appio, F.P., & Mora, L. (2019). The advent of practice theories in research on sustainable consumption: Past, current and future directions of the field. *Sustainability*, 11(341), 1–19.

Cornwell, B., Chi Cui, C., Mitchell, V., Schlegelmilch, B., Dzulkiflee, A., & Chan, J. (2005). A cross-cultural study of the role of religion in consumers' ethical positions. *International Marketing Review*, 22(5), 531–546.

Cova, B. & Cova, V. (2012). On the road to prosumption: Marketing discourse and the development of consumer competencies, *Consumption Markets & Culture*, 115(2), 149–168.

Creyer, E.H., & Ross, W.T. (1997). The influence of firm behaviour on purchase intention: do consumers really care about business ethics? *Journal of Consumer Marketing*, 14(6), 421–432.

Dauvergne, P., & Lister, J. (2010). The prospects and limits of eco-consumerism: Shopping our way to less deforestation. *Organization and Environment*, 23(2), 132–154.

Davies, I., Lee, Z., & Ahonkhai, I. (2012). Do consumers care about ethical-luxury? *Journal of Business Ethics*, 106, 37–51.

Davies, I.A., & Gutsche, S. (2016). Consumer motivations for mainstream "ethical" consumption. *European Journal of Marketing*, 50(7/8), 1326–1347.

DEFRA (2008). *A Framework for Pro-environmental Behaviours*. January 2008 [online]. Available at: http://www.defra.gov.uk/evidence/social/behaviour/ pdf/behaviours-jan08-report.pdf. [Accessed 5 January 2015].

De Groot, J.I.M., Schubert, I., & Thøgersen, J. (2016). 'Morality and Green Consumer Behaviour: A Psychological Perspective'. In: *Ethics and Morality in Consumption: Interdisciplinary Perspectives*. D. Shaw, A. Chatzidakis and M. Carrington (eds.). London: Routledge.

De Groot, J.I.M., & Steg, L. (2010). Relationships between value orientations, self-determined motivational types and pro-environmental behavioural intentions. *Journal of Environmental Psychology*, 30, 368–378.

Deng, X., & Xu, Y. (2017). Consumers' responses to corporate social responsibility initiatives: The mediating role of consumer–company identification. *Journal of Business Ethics*, 142, 515–526.

Denni, A., & Pekerti, A. (2017). Who is more ethical? Cross-cultural comparison of consumer ethics between religious and non-religious consumers. *Journal of Consumer Behaviour*, 16(1), 82–98.

De Pelsmacker, P., Driesen, L., & Rayp, G. (2005). Do consumers care about ethics? Willingness to pay for fair-trade coffee. *Journal of Consumer Affairs, 39*(2), 363–385.

de Spiegeleer, J., Höcht, S., Jakubowski, D., Reyners, S., & Schoutens, W. (2022). ESG: A new dimension in portfolio allocation. *Journal of Sustainable Finance & Investment* [online: ahead of print]. DOI: 10.1080/20430795.2021.1923336

Devinney, T.M., Auger, P., & Eckhardt, G.M. (2010). *The Myth of the Ethical Consumer.* Cambridge: Cambridge University Press.

Dianati, S., & Banfield, G. (2020). Business as usual: Critical management studies and the case of environmental sustainability education. *Journal for Critical Education Policy Studies, 18*(2), 325–357.

Dickson, M.A. (2005). 'Identifying and Profiling Apparel Label Users'. *In:* R. Harrison, T. Newholm and D. Shaw (eds.). *The Ethical Consumer.* London: Sage Publications.

Djafarova, E., & Foots, S. (2022). Exploring ethical consumption of Generation Z: theory of planned behaviour. *Young Consumers* [online: ahead of print]. https://doi.org/10.1108/YC-10-2021-1405

Earle, A.G., & Leyva-de la Hiz, D.I. (2020). The wicked problem of teaching about wicked problems: Design thinking and emerging technologies in sustainability education. *Management Learning, 52*(5), 581–603.

Eckhardt, G.M., Belk, R., & Devinney, T.M. (2010). Why don't consumers consume ethically? *Journal of Consumer Behaviour, 9* (Nov–Dec), 426–436.

Edelman (2021). *Edelman Trust Barometer 2021: Global Report* [online]. Available at: www.edelman.com/sites/g/files/aatuss191/files/2021-03/2021%20Edelman%20Trust%20Barometer.pdf

Elkington, J. (1999). *Cannibals With Forks: The Triple Bottom Line of 21st Century Business.* Oxford: Capstone Publishing.

Firat, A.F., Dholakia, N., & Venkatesh, A. (1995). Marketing in a postmodern world. *European Journal of Marketing, 29*(1), 40–56.

Fishbein, M., & Ajzen, I. (2010). *Belief, Attitude, Intention and Behavior: An Introduction to Theory and Research.* Reading, MA: Addison-Wesley, p.6.

Fisher, J. (2004). Social responsibility and ethics: Clarifying the concepts. *Journal of Business Ethics, 52*, 391–400.

Fisher, T., Cooper, T., Woodward, S., Hiller, A., & Goworek, H. (2008). Public Understanding of Sustainable Clothing: A report to the Department for Environment, Food and Rural Affairs. London: DEFRA.

Francis, T., & Hoefl, F. (2018). *True Gen: Generation Z and its Implications for Companies.* McKinsey and Company [online]. Available at: www.mckinsey.com/~/media/McKinsey/Industries/Consumer%20Packaged%20Goods/Our%20Insights/True%20Gen%20Generation%20Z%20and%20its%20implications%20for%20companies/Generation-Z-and-its-implication-for-companies.pdf

Gallarza, M.G., Arteaga, F., Del Chiappa, G., Gil-Saura, I., & Holbrook, M.B. (2017). A multidimensional service-value scale based on Holbrook's typology of customer value: Bridging the gap between the concept and its measurement. *Journal of Service Management, 28*(4), 724–764.

Gabriel, Y., & Lang, T. (2006). *The Unmanageable Consumer* (2nd ed). London: Sage.

Garcia-Ruiz, P., & Rodriguez-Lluesma, C. (2014). Consumption practices: A virtue ethics approach. *Business Ethics Quarterly*, *24*(4), 509–531.

Giddens, A. (1991). *Modernity and Identity: Self and Society in the Late Modern Age*. Cambridge. Polity Press.

Giesler, M., & Veresiu, E. (2014). Creating the responsible consumer: Moralistic governance regimes and consumer subjectivity. *Journal of Consumer Research*, *41*(October), 840–857.

Glac, K. (2009). Understanding socially responsible investing: The effect of decision frames and trade-off options. *Journal of Business Ethics*, *87*(Supplement 1), 41–55.

Godwin, M.P. (2009). Conscious consumerism: The cash value of values. *Ethics and Critical Thinking Journal*, *85*, 3–10.

Goulding, C., Shankar, A., & Canniford, R. (2013). Learning to be tribal: Facilitating the formation of consumer tribes. *European Journal of Marketing*, *47*(5/6), 813–832.

Govind, R., Singh, J.J., & Garg, N. (2019). Not walking the walk: How dual attitudes influence behavioral outcomes in ethical consumption. *Journal of Business Ethics*, *155*, 1195–1214.

Gregory-Smith, D., Smith, A., & Winlhofer, H. (2013). Emotions and dissonance in 'ethical' consumption choices. *Journal of Marketing Management*, *29*(11–12), 1201–1223.

Griffiths, P. (2011). Ethical objections to fairtrade. *Journal of Business Ethics*, *105*, 357–373.

Gummerus, J. (2013). Value creation processes and value outcomes in marketing theory: Strangers or siblings? *Marketing Theory*, *13*(1), 19–46.

Gummerus, J., Liljander, V., & Sihlman, R. (2017). Do ethical social media communities pay off? An exploratory study of the ability of Facebook ethical communities to strengthen consumers' ethical consumption behavior. *Journal of Business Ethics*, *144*, 449–465.

Gutman, J. (1982). A means–end chain model based on consumer categorisation processes. *Journal of Marketing*, *46*(Spring), 60–72.

Ha-Brookshire, J.E., & Norum, P.S. (2011). Willingness to pay for socially responsible products: A case of cotton apparel. *Journal of Consumer Marketing*, *28*(5), 344–353.

Halkier, B., Katz-Gerro, T., & Martens, L. (2011). Applying practice theory to the study of consumption: Theoretical and methodological considerations. *Journal of Consumer Culture*, *11*(1), 3–13.

Han, T-I., & Stoel, L. (2017) Explaining socially responsible consumer behavior: A meta-analytic review of theory of planned behavior. *Journal of International Consumer Marketing*, *29*(2), 91–103.

Hargreaves, T. (2011). Practiceing behavior change: applying social practice theory to pro-environmental behavior change. *Journal of Consumer Culture*, *11*(1), 79–99.

Hassan, L., Shaw, D., Shiu, E., Walsh, G., & Pary, S. (2013). Uncertainty in ethical consumer choice: a conceptual model. *Journal of Consumer Behaviour*, *12*, 182–193.

Hassan, S.M., Rahman, Z. & Paul, J. (2021). Consumer ethics: a review and research agenda. *Psychology and Marketing*, *39*(1), 111–130.

Hassan, L., Shiu, E., & Shaw, D. (2016). Who says there is an intention-behaviour gap? *Journal of Business Ethics*, *136*(2), 219–236.

Hawkins, R. (2012). A new frontier in development? The use of cause-related marketing by international development organisations. *Third World Quarterly*, *33*(10), 1783–1801.

Heath, J., & Potter, A. (2006). *The Rebel Sell: How the Counterculture Became Consumer Culture*. Chichester: Capstone Publishing.

Heinonen, K., Strandvik, T., & Voima, P. (2013). Customer dominant value formation in service. *European Business Review*, *25*(2), 104–123.

Helkkula, A., Kelleher, C., & Pihlström, M. (2012). Characterizing value as an experience: Implications for service researchers and managers. *Journal of Service Research*, *15*(1), 59–75.

Heskett, J.L., Jones, T.O., Loveman, G.W., Sasser Jr, W.E., & Schlesinger, L.A. (1994). Putting the service-profit chain to work. *Harvard Business Review*, *72*(2), 164–174.

Hiller, A., & Woodall, T. (2019). Everything flows: A pragmatist perspective of trade-offs and value in ethical consumption. *Journal of Business Ethics*, *157*(4), 893–912.

Hiller Connell, K.Y. (2010). Internal and external barriers to eco-conscious apparel acquisition. *International Journal of Consumer Studies*, *34*, 279–286.

Hinman, L.M. (2003). *Ethics: A Pluralistic Approach to Moral Theory* (3rd ed.). Belmont: Wadsworth/Thomson Learning.

Hoelscher, V., & Chatzidakis, A. (2021). Ethical consumption communities across physical and digital spaces: An exploration of their complementary and synergistic affordances. *Journal of Business Ethics*, *172*(2), 291–306.

Hohnen, P., & Potts, J. (2007). *Corporate Social responsibility: An Implementation Guide for Business*. International Institute for Sustainable Development [online]. Available at: www.iisd.org/system/files?file=publications/csr_gu ide.pdf

Holbrook, M.B. (1994). The nature of customer value: An axiology of services in the consumption experience. *Service Quality: New Directions in Theory and Practice*, *21*, 21–71.

Huddart Kennedy, E., Cohen, M.J., & Krogman N.T. (2015). 'Social Practice Theories and Research on Sustainable Consumption'. *In*: Emily Huddart Kennedy and Maurie J. Cohen (eds.). *Putting Sustainability into Practice: Applications and Advances in Research on Sustainable Consumption*. Naomi Krogman: Edward Elgar Publishing.

Hughes, A., Buttle, M., & Wrigley, N. (2007). Organisational geographies of corporate responsibility: a UK–US comparison of retailers' ethical trading initiatives. *Journal of Economic Geography*, *7*(4), 491–513.

Hustvedt, G., & Dickson, M.A. (2009). Consumer likelihood of purchasing organic cotton apparel: Influence of attitudes and self-identity. *Journal of Fashion Marketing and Management, 13*(1), 49–65.

Hyllegard, K., Ogle, J., & Yan, R-N. (2009). The impact of advertising message strategy–fair labour v. sexual appeal–upon Gen Y consumers' intent to patronize an apparel retailer. *Journal of Fashion Marketing and Management, 13*(1), 109–127.

Inglehart, R., & Welzel, C. (2005). *Modernisation, Cultural Change and Democracy: The Human Development Sequence.* Cambridge: Cambridge University Press.

Iwanow, H., McEachern, M.G., & Jeffrey, A. (2005). The influence of ethical trading policies on consumer apparel purchase decisions. A focus on The Gap Inc. *International Journal of Retail and Distribution Management, 33*(5), 371–387.

Jackson, T. (2005). *Motivating Sustainable Consumption: A Review of Evidence on Consumer Behaviour and Behavioural Change.* University of Surrey: Centre for Environmental Strategy.

Jägel, T., Keeling, K., Reppel, A., & Gruber, T. (2012). Individual values and motivational complexities in ethical clothing consumption: A means–end approach. *Journal of Marketing Management, 28*(3–4), 373–396.

Janssen, C., & Vanhamme, J. (2015). Theoretical lenses for understanding the CSR-consumer paradox. *Journal of Business Ethics, 130*(4), 775.

Jayawardhena, C., Morrell, K., & Stride, C. (2016). Ethical consumption behaviours in supermarket shoppers: Determinants and marketing implications. *Journal of Marketing Management, 32*(7–8), 777–805.

Joergens, C. (2006). Ethical fashion: Myth or future trend? *Journal of Fashion Marketing and Management, 10*(3), 360–371.

Johnstone, M-L., & Tan, L.P. (2015). Exploring the gap between consumers' green rhetoric and purchasing behaviour. *Journal of Business Ethics, 132*(2), 311–328.

Johnstone, M-L. & Hooper, S. (2016). Social influence and green consumption behaviour: A need for greater government involvement. *Journal of Marketing Management, 32*(9–10), 827–855.

Kahle, L.R., & Kennedy, P. (1988). Using the list of values (LOV) to understand consumers. *The Journal of Services Marketing, 2*(4), 49–56.

Kim, G.S., Lee, G.Y., &Park, K. (2010). A cross-national investigation on how ethical consumers build loyalty towards fair trade brands. *Journal of Business Ethics, 96*, 589–611.

Kim, S., Littrell, M.A., & Paff Ogle, J.L. (1999). The relative importance of social responsibility as a predictor of purchase intentions for clothing. *Journal of Fashion Marketing and Management, 3*(3), 207–218.

Kincaid, D.H., Giddings, V.L., and Chen-Yu, J. (1998). Impact of product-specific variables on consumers' post-consumption behaviour for apparel products: USA. *Journal of Consumer Studies and Home Economics, 22*(2), 81–90.

Knowles, J., Hunsaker, B.T., Grove, H., & James, A. (2022). What is the purpose of your purpose? *Harvard Business Review*. March–April.

Kozinets, R.V., & Handelman, J. (1998). Ensouling consumption: A netnographic exploration of the meaning of boycotting behaviour. *Advances in Consumer Research*, *25*, 475–480.

Kuokkanen, H., & Sun, W. (2020). Companies, meet ethical consumers: Strategic CSR management to impact consumer choice. *Journal of Business Ethics*, *166*, 403–423.

Lages, L.F., & Fernandes, J.C. (2004). The SERPVAL scale: A multi-item instrument for measuring service personal values. *Journal of Business Research*, *58*(2), 1562–1572.

Lee, K-H., Scott, N., & Packer, J. (2014). Habitus and slow food lifestyle: In-destination activity participation of Slow Food members. *Annals of Tourism Research*, 48, 207–220.

Lim, W.M., Yong, J.L.S., & Suryadi, K. (2014). Consumers' perceived value and willingness to purchase organic food. *Journal of Global Marketing*, *27*, 298–307.

Lin, Y.L., & Lin, H.W. (2015). The benefits and values of green lifestyle consumers. *International Journal of Marketing Studies*, *7*(1), 24–38.

Littler, J. (2011). 'What's Wrong with Ethical Consumption?' *In:* T. Lewis, and E. Potter (eds.). *Ethical Consumption: A Critical Introduction*. London: Routledge. pp.27–39.

Littrell, M.A., Ma, Y.J, & Halepete, J. (2005). Generation X, baby boomers, and swing: marketing fair trade apparel. *Journal of Fashion Marketing and Management*, *9*(4), 407–419.

Longo, C., Shankar, A., & Nuttall, P. (2017). "It's not easy living a sustainable lifestyle": How greater knowledge leads to dilemmas, tensions and paralysis. *Journal of Business Ethics*. Online ahead of print, DOI: 10.1007/s10551-016-3422-1

Low, W., & Davenport, E. (2005). Has the medium (roast) become the message? The ethics of marketing fair trade in the mainstream. *International Marketing Review*, *22*(5), 494–511.

Low, W., & Davenport, E. (2007). To boldly go… exploring ethical spaces to re-politicise ethical consumption and fair trade. *Journal of Consumer Behaviour*, 6(Sept/Oct), 336–348.

Lu, L-C., Chang, H-H., & Chong, A. (2015). Consumer personality and green buying intention: The mediate role of consumer ethical beliefs. *Journal of Business Ethics*, *127*, 205–219.

Luchs, M.G., & Kumar, M. (2017). "Yes, but this other one looks better/works better": How do consumers respond to trade-offs between sustainability and other valued attributes? *Journal of Business Ethics*, *140*(3), 567–584.

Luedicke, M.K., Thompson, C.J., & Giesler, M. (2009). Consumer identity work as moral protagonism: How myth and identity animate a brand-mediated moral conflict. *Journal of Consumer Research*, *36*(April), 1016–1032.

Lundblad, L., & Davies, I.A. (2016). The values and motivations behind sustainable fashion consumption. *Journal of Consumer Behaviour*, *15*(2), 149–162.

Luo, X., & Bhattacharya, C.B. (2006). Corporate social responsibility, customer satisfaction and market value. *Journal of Marketing, 70*(October), 1–18.

Ma, Y.J., Littrell, M.A., & Niehm, L. (2012). Young female consumers' intentions toward fair trade consumption. *International Journal of Retail and Distribution Management, 40*(1), 41–63.

Mahoney, J. (1994). What makes a business company ethical? *Business Strategy Review, 5*(4), 1–15.

Malone, S., McCabe, S., & Smith, A.P. (2014). The role of hedonism in ethical tourism. *Annals of Tourism Research, 44*, 241–254.

Manchiraju, S., & Sadachar, A. (2014). Personal values and ethical fashion consumption. *Journal of Fashion Marketing and Management, 18*(3), 357–374.

Markkula, A., & Moisander, J. (2012). Discursive confusion over sustainable consumption: A discursive perspective on the perplexity of marketplace knowledge. *Journal of Consumer Policy, 35*(1), 105–125.

Mazar, N., & Zhong, C-B. (2009). *Do Green Products Make Us Better People?* [online]. Available at: www.rotman.utoronto.ca/newthinking/greenproducts.pdf. [Accessed 6 November 2009].

McDonald, S., Oates, C.J., Alevizou, P.J., Young W.C., & Hwang, K. (2012). Individual strategies for sustainable consumption, *Journal of Marketing Management, 28*(3–4), 445-468.

McGoldrick, P.J., & Freestone, O.M. (2008). Ethical product premiums: Antecedents and extent of consumers' willingness to pay. *The International Journal of Retail, Distribution and Consumer Research, 18*(2), 185–201.

McShane, T.O., Hirsch, P.D., Trung, T.C., Songorwa, A.N., Kinzig, A., Monteferri, B., Mutekanga, D., Van Thang, H., Dammert, J.L., Pulgar-Vidal, M., Welch-Devine, M., Brosius, J.P., Coppolillo, P., & O'Connor, S. (2011). Hard choices: Making trade-offs between biodiversity conservation and human well-being. *Biological Conservation, 144*(3), 966–972.

Memery, J., Megicks, P., & Williams, J. (2005). Ethical and social responsibility issues in grocery shopping: A preliminary typology. *Qualitative Market Research: An International Journal, 8*(4), 399–412.

Millar, J. & Price, M. (2018). Imagining management education: A critique of the contribution of the United Nations PRME to critical reflexivity and rethinking management education. *Management Learning, 49*(3), 346–362.

Miller, D. (2012). *Consumption and its Consequences*. Cambridge: Polity Press.

Mintel (2022a). *Consumer Trends, Attitudes and Spending Habits for the Home–UK 2022*. Mintel: London.

Mintel (2022b). *Sports Goods Retailing–UK 2022*. Mintel: London.

Mintel (2022c). *Menswear–UK 2022*. Mintel: London.

Mish, J. & Miller, A. (2014). 'Marketing's Contributions to a Sustainable Society.' *In:* P.E. Murphy and J.F. Sherry Jr (eds.). *Marketing and the Common Good: Essays from Notre Dame on Societal Impact*. Abingdon: Routledge. pp.153–174.

Mohr, L.A., & Webb, D.J. (2005). The effects of social responsibility and price on consumer responses. *Journal of Consumer Affairs, 39*(1), 121–147.

Moisander, J. (2007). Motivational complexity of green consumerism. *International Journal of Consumer Studies*, *31*(4), 404–409.

Monbiot, G. (2009). *We Cannot Change the World by Changing Our Buying Habits*. The Guardian [online]. Available at: www.guardian.co.uk/envi ronment/georgemonbiot/2009/nov/06/green-consumerism. [Accessed 6 November 2009].

Moor, L., & Littler, J. (2008). Fourth worlds and Neo-Fordism. *Cultural Studies*, *22*(5), 700–723.

Moores, T.T., & Chang, J.C.-J. (2006). Ethical decision making in software piracy: Initial development and test of a four-component model. *MIS Quarterly*, *30*(1), 167–180.

Moraes, C., Carrigan, M., Bosangit, C., Ferreira, C., & McGrath, M. (2017). Understanding ethical luxury consumption through practice theories: A study of fine jewellery purchases. *Journal of Business Ethics*, *145*, 525–543.

Moraes, C., Carrigan, M., & Szmigin, I. (2012). The coherence of inconsisten- cies: Attitude–behaviour gaps and new consumption communities. *Journal of Marketing Management*, *28*(1–2), 103–128.

Moraes, C., Shaw, D., & Carrigan, M. (2011). Purchase power: An examination of consumption as voting. *Journal of Marketing Management*, *27*(9–10), 1059–1079.

Neville, S. (2015). Benetton contributes to UN-fund for victims of garment fac- tory collapse. *The Independent*, 20 February [online]. Available at: www.inde pendent.co.uk/news/business/news/benetton-contributes-to-unfund-for-vict ims-of-garment-factory-collapse-10060323.html

Newholm, T. (2005). 'Case Studying Ethical Consumers' Projects and Strategies.' *In:* R. Harrison, T. Newholm and D. Shaw (eds.). *The Ethical Consumer*. London: Sage Publications.

Newholm, T., Newholm, S., & Shaw, D. (2015). A history for consumption ethics. *Business History*, *57*(2), 290–310.

Newholm, T., & Shaw, D. (2007). Editorial. Studying the ethical consumer: A review of research. *Journal of Consumer Behaviour*, *6*(Sept–Oct), 253–270.

Ng, I.C.L., & Smith, L.A. (2012). 'An Integrative Framework of Value.' *In:* Vargo, S.L, and Lusch, R.F. *Review of Marketing Research, Special Issue: Toward a Better Understanding of the Role of Value in Markets and Marketing*. Bingley: Emerald Group Publishing.

Nicholls, A., & Opal, C., 2005. *Fair Trade: Market-Driven Ethical Consumption*. London: Sage Publications Ltd.

OECD (2009). 'Overview of Selected Initiatives and Instruments Relevant to Corporate Social Responsibility.' *In: Annual Report on the OECD Guidelines for Multinational Enterprises 2008*. Paris: Organisation for Economic Co-Operation and Development. www.oecd.org/corporate/ mne/40889288.pdf

Painter, M., Hibbert, S., & Cooper, T (2019). The development of responsible and sustainable business practice: Value, mind-sets, business-models. *Journal of Business Ethics*, *157*(4), 885–891.

Painter-Morland, M. (2011). *Business Ethics as Practice*. Cambridge: Cambridge University Press.

Painter-Morland, M., Sabet, E., Molthan-Hill, P., Goworek, H., & de Leeuw, S. (2016). Beyond the curriculum: Integrating sustainability into business schools. *Journal of Business Ethics*. https://doi.org/10.1007/s10 551-015-2896-6

Papaoikonomou, E., & Alarcón A. (2017). Revisiting consumer empowerment: An exploration of ethical consumption communities. *Journal of Macromarketing, 37*(1), 40–56.

Papaoikonomou, E., Ryan, G., & Ginieis, M. (2011). Towards a holistic approach of the attitude–behavior gap in ethical consumer behaviors: Empirical evidence from Spain. *International Advances in Economic Research, 17*, 77–88.

Paul, M., Hennig-Thurau, T., Gremler, D.D., Gwinner, K.P., & Wiertz, C. (2009). Toward a theory of repeat purchase drivers for consumer services. *Journal of the Academy of Marketing Science, 37*, 215–237.

Pecoraro, M., Uusitalo, O., & Valtonen, A. (2021). Experiencing ethical retail ideology in the servicescape. *Journal of Marketing Management, 37*, 5–6, 520–547.

Perera, C., Auger, P. & Klein, J. (2018). Green consumption practices among young environmentalists: A practice theory perspective. *Journal of Business Ethics, 152*, 843–864.

Petro, G. (2020). 'Sustainable Retail: How Gen Z Is Leading the Pack'. *Forbes*. 31 January [online]. Available at: www.forbes.com/sites/gregpetro/2020/01/31/sustainable-retail-how-gen-z-is-leading-the-pack/?sh=1d24bd512ca3

Phipps, M., Ozanne, L.K., Luchs, M.G., Subrahmanyan, S., Kapitan, S., Catlin, J.R., Gau, R., Naylor, R.W., Rose, R.L., Simpson, B., & Weaver, T. (2013). Understanding the inherent complexity of sustainable consumption: A social cognitive framework. *Journal of Business Research, 66*(8), 1227–1234.

Pinna, M. (2019). Do gender identities of femininity and masculinity affect the intention to buy ethical products? *Psychology and Marketing, 37*(3), 384–397.

Pinto, D.C., Herter, M.M., Rossi, P., & Borges, A. (2014). Going green for self or for others? Gender and identity salience effects on sustainable consumption. *International Journal of Consumer Studies, 38*(5), 540–549.

Pivato, S., Misani, N., & Tencati, A. (2008). The impact of corporate social responsibility on consumer trust: The case of organic food. *Business Ethics: A European Review, 17*(1), 3–12.

Ramasamy, B., Yeung, M.C.H., & Au, A.K.M. (2010). Consumer support for corporate social responsibility: The role of religion and values. *Journal of Business Ethics, 91*, 61–72.

Rawwas, M., & Singhapakdi, A. (1998). Do consumers' ethical beliefs vary with age? A substantiation of Kohlberg's typology in marketing. *Journal of Marketing Theory and Practice*, Spring, 26–38.

Robichaud, Z., & Yu, H. (2021). Do young consumers care about ethical consumption? Modelling Gen Z's purchase intention towards fair trade coffee. *British Food Journal* [online]. DOI 10.1108/BFJ-05-2021-0536

Rokeach, M. (1973). *The Nature of Human Values.* New York: The Free Press.

Røpke, I. (2009). Theories of practice – new inspiration for ecological economic studies on consumption. *Ecological Economics, 68*(10), 2490–2497.

Rorty, R. (1995). 'Dewey Between Hegel and Darwin.' *In*: H.J. SAATKAMP Jr. (1995) (Ed.). *Rorty and Pragmatism.* Nashville: Vanderbilt University Press. pp.1–15.

Sanchez-Fernandez, R., Iniesta-Bonillo, M.A., & Holbrook, M.B. (2009). The conceptualisation and measurement of consumer value in services. *International Journal of Market Research, 51*(1), 93–113.

Schaefer, A., & Crane, A. (2005). Addressing sustainability and consumption. *Journal of Macromarketing, 25*(1), 76–92.

Schlegelmilch, B.B., Bohlen, G.M., & Diamantopoulos, A. (1996). The link between green purchasing decisions and measures of environmental consciousness. *European Journal of Marketing, 30*(5), 35–55.

Schmitt, B., Brakus, J.J., & Biraglia, A. (2022). Consumption ideology. *Journal of Consumer Research, 49*(1), 74–95.

Schmuck, D., Matthes, J., & Naderer, B. (2018). Misleading consumers with green advertising? An affect–reason–involvement account of greenwashing effects in environmental advertising. *Journal of Advertising, 47*(2), 127–145.

Schröder, M.J.A., & McEachern, M. (2004). Consumer value conflicts surrounding ethical food purchase decisions: A focus on animal welfare. *International Journal of Consumer Studies, 28*(2), 168–177.

Schwartz, D.T. (2010). *Consuming Choices: Ethics in a Global Consumer Age.* Plymouth: Rowman and Littlefield.

Schwartz, M.S., & Carroll, A.B. (2003). Corporate social responsibility: A three-domain approach. *Business Ethics Quarterly, 13*(4), 503–530.

Schwartz, S.H. (1994). Are there universal aspects in the structure and contents of human values? *Journal of Social Issues, 50*(4), 19–45.

Schwartz, S.H. (2009). *Basic Human Values* [online]. Available at: http://ccsr.ac.uk/qmss/seminars/2009-06-10/documents/Shalom_Schwartz_1.pdf. [Accessed 28 August 2012].

Sebastiani, R., Montagnini, F., & Dalli, D. (2013). Ethical consumption and new business models in the food industry. Evidence from the Eataly case. *Journal of Business Ethics, 114*(3), 473–488.

Shang, J., & Peloza, J. (2016). Can "real" men consume ethically? How ethical consumption leads to unintended observer inference. *Journal of Business Ethics, 139*(1), 129–145.

Shankar, A., Elliott, R., & Fitchett, J.A. (2009). Identity, consumption and narratives of socialisation. *Marketing Theory, 9*(1), 75–94.

Shaw, D., & Clarke, I. (1999). Belief formation in ethical consumer groups: An exploratory study. *Marketing Intelligence and Planning, 17*(2), 109–119.

Shaw, D., Grehan, E., Shiu, E., Hassan, L., & Thomson, J. (2005). An exploration of values in ethical consumer decision making. *Journal of Consumer Behaviour, 4*(3), 185–200.

Shaw, D., Hogg, G., Wilson, E., Shui, E., & Hassan, L. (2006). Fashion victim: The impact of fair trade concerns on clothing choice. *Journal of Strategic Marketing, 14,* 427–440.

Shaw, D., & Riach, K. (2011). Embracing ethical fields: Constructing consumption in the margins. *European Journal of Marketing, 45*(7/8), 1051–1067.

Shaw, D., Shiu, E., & Clarke, I. (2000). The contribution of ethical obligation and self-identity to the theory of planned behaviour: An exploration of ethical consumers. *Journal of Marketing Management, 16*(8), 879–894.

Shaw, D., Shui E., Hassan, L., Bekin, C., & Hogg, G. (2007). Intending to be ethical: An examination of consumer choice in sweatshop avoidance. *Advances in Consumer Research, 34,* 31–38.

Shephard, K. (2008). Higher education for sustainability: Seeking affective learning outcomes. *International Journal of Sustainability in Higher Education, 9*(1), 87–98.

Sheppard, B.H., Hartwick, J., & Warshaw, P.R. (1988). The theory of reasoned action: A meta-analysis of past research with recommendations for modifications and future research. *Journal of Consumer Research, 15*(Dec), 325–343.

Shiu, E.M.K., Walsh, G., Hassan, L., & Shaw, D. (2011). Consumer uncertainty, revisited. *Psychology and Marketing, 28*(6), 584–607.

Shove, E. (2010). Beyond the ABC: Climate change policy and theories of social change. *Environment and Planning, 42*(6), 1273–1285.

Sims, R.L., & Gegez, A.E. (2004). Attitudes towards business ethics: A five nation comparative study. *Journal of Business Ethics, 50,* 253–265.

Skålén, P., Pace, S., & Cova, B. (2015). Firm-brand community value co-creation as alignment of practices. *European Journal of Marketing, 49*(3/4), 596–620.

Smith, N.C. (1999). 'Ethics and the typology of consumer value.' *In*: M.B. Holbrook (ed). *Consumer Value: A Framework for Research and Analysis.* London: Routledge.

Sparks, P., & Shepherd, R. (1992). Self-identity and the theory of planned behaviour: Assessing the role of identification with 'green consumerism'. *Social Psychology Quarterly, 55*(4), 388–399.

Sreen, N., Purbey, S., & Sadarangani, P. (2018). Impact of culture, behavior and gender on green purchase intention. *Journal of Retailing and Consumer Services, 41,* 177–189.

Stern, P.C. (2000). Towards a coherent theory of environmentally significant behaviour. *Journal of Social Issues, 56*(3), 407–424.

Stobierski, T. (2021). *Types of Corporate Social Responsibility to Be Aware of.* Harvard Business School Business Insights [online]. Available at: https://online.hbs.edu/blog/post/types-of-corporate-social-responsibility. [Accessed 16 May 2022].

Straughan, R.D., & Roberts, J.A. (1999). Environmental segmentation alternatives: a look at green consumer behavior in the new millennium. *Journal of Consumer Marketing, 16*(6), 558–575.

Strong, C. (1997). The problems of translating fair trade principles into consumer purchase behaviour. *Marketing Intelligence and Planning, 15*(1), 32–37.

Sun, W. (2019). Toward a theory of ethical consumer intention formation: re-extending the theory of planned behaviour. *AMS Review, 10*, 260–278.

Szmigin, I., & Carrigan, M. (2006). Exploring the dimensions of ethical consumption. *European Advances in Consumer Research, 7*, 608–613.

Szmigin, I., Carrigan, M., & McEachern, M. (2009). The conscious consumer: Taking a flexible approach to ethical behaviour. *International Journal of Consumer Studies, 33*(2), 224–231.

Tadajewski, M., & Wagner-Tsukamoto, S. (2006). Anthropology and consumer research: qualitative insights into green consumer behavior. *Qualitative Market Research: An International Journal, 9*(1), 8–25.

Tarrant, S.P., & Thiele, L.P (2016). Practice makes pedagogy: John Dewey and skills-based sustainability education. *International Journal of Sustainability in Higher Education, 17*(1), 54–67.

The Economist (2006). Good food? *The Economist.* December 9, p11. www.economist.com/leaders/2006/12/07/good-food

Thompson, C.J., Arnould, E., & Giesler, M. (2013). Discursivity, difference and disruption: Genealogical reflections on the consumer culture heteroglossia. *Marketing Theory, 13*(2), 149–174.

Thøgersen, J. (1996). Recycling and morality: A critical review of the literature. *Environment and Behavior, 28*(4), 536–558.

Tynan, C., McKechnie, S., & Hartley, S. (2014). Interpreting value in the customer service experience using customer-dominant logic. *Journal of Marketing Management, 30*(9–10), 1058–1081.

Udell, A.M., de Groot, J.I.M., de Jong, S., & Shankar, A. (2020). How do I see myself? A systematic review if identities in pro-environmental behaviour research. *Journal of Consumer Behaviour,* 1–34.

Valor, C. (2007). The influence of information about labour abuses on consumer choice of clothes: A grounded theory approach. *Journal of Marketing Management, 23*(7–8), 675–695.

Valor, C. (2008). Can consumers buy responsibly? Analysis and solutions for market failures. *Journal of Consumer Policy, 31*, 315–326.

Vargo, S.L., & Lusch, R.F. (2004). Evolving to a new dominant logic for marketing. *Journal of Marketing, 68*(1), 1–17.

Vargo, S.L, & Lusch, R.F. (2008). Service dominant logic: continuing the evolution. *Journal of the Academy of Marketing Science, 36*, 1–10.

Vargo, S.L, & Lusch, R.F. (2012). 'The Nature and Understanding of Value: A Service-Dominant Logic Perpsective.' *In:* S.L. Vargo, and R.F. Lusch (eds.). *Review of Marketing Research, Special Issue: Toward a Better Understanding of the Role of Value in Markets and Marketing.* Bingley: Emerald Group Publishing.

Vitell, S.J., & Muncy, J. (2005). The Muncy-Vitell Scale: A modification and application. *Journal of Business Ethics, 62,* 267–275.

Vitell, S.J., & Paolillo, J.G.P. (2004). A cross-cultural study of the antecedents of the perceived role of ethics and social responsibility. *Business Ethics: A European Review, 13* (2/3), 185–199.

Wagner, S.A. (2003). *Understanding Green Consumer Behaviour: A Qualitative Cognitive Approach.* London: Routledge.

Warde, A. (2005). Consumption and theories of practice. *Journal of Consumer Culture, 5*(2), 131–153.

Warde, A. (2014). After taste: Culture, consumption and theories of practice. *Journal of Consumer Culture, 14*(3), 279–303.

White, K., Macdonnell, R., & Ellard, J.H. (2012). Belief in a just world: Consumer intentions and behaviours towards ethical products. *Journal of Marketing, 76,* 103–118.

Wiggins, D. (2006). *Ethics: Twelve Lectures on the Philosophy of Morality.* London: Penguin.

Wilson, A. (2007). Rising to the challenge: How to develop responsible leaders. *Leadership in Action, 27,* 7–11.

Worcester, R., & Dawkins, J. (2005). 'Surveying Ethical and Environmental Attitudes.' *In:* R. Harrison, T. Newholm and D. Shaw (eds.). *The Ethical Consumer.* London: Sage Publications.

Woodall, T., Hiller, A., & Resnick, S. (2014). Making sense of higher education: Students as consumers and the value of the university experience. *Studies in Higher Education, 39*(1), 48–67.

Zagata, L. (2014). Towards conscientious food consumption: Exploring the values of Czech organic food consumers. *International Journal of Consumer Studies, 38*(3), 243–250.

Zeithaml, V.A. (1988). Consumer perceptions of price, quality, and value: A means–end model and synthesis of evidence. *The Journal of Marketing, 52*(3), 2–22.

Zeno Group (2020). *2020 Zeno Strength of Purpose Study* [online]. Available at: https://drive.google.com/file/d/1ni3dl4jAEWn7d0KxD_-rB05p2ZoBJ JlC/view

Zollo, L. (2021). The consumers' emotional dog learns to persuade its rational tail: Toward a social intuitionist framework of ethical consumption. *Journal of Business Ethics, 168*(2), 295–313.

Index

Note: Page numbers in **bold** denote tables.

Abrantes Ferreira, D. 34, 57
Accenture 12
activism 1, 4, 6, 11
Acuti, D. 54
Aertsens, J. 35
Agag, G. **17**, 19
age 17–18
Ajzen, I. 26, 27–8
Alarcón, A. 42
Allen, S. 61
Alsaad, A. **17**, 19
ambivalence 34, 52, 56, 60
Anderson, W.T. 16–17
animals 5, 24, 48
anti-consumerism 6
Antonetti, P. 54–5
Arli, D. **17**, 19–20
Arnould, E.J. 38, 41, 56
Arsel, Z. 42
Attalla, A. 48, 50, 51
attitude–behaviour gap 51–3, 59
awareness 48–51

Babakus, E. **17**, 20
Balabanis, G. 56
Banfield, G. 10, 61
Bartels, J. 28, 38, 39, 41, 42
Baudrillard, J. 30
Bauman, Z. 39, 41, 60
Baumber, A. 61
B-Corp movement 7
Belk, R.W. 38
Bhattacharya, C.B. 56

Birch, S. 13
Bloemer, J. 32
Bly, S. 44
Bourdieu, P. 43–4
boycotts 1, 4, 5, 6
Bray, J. 49, 52, 53, 54
Brinkmann, J. 11, 15
Brown, S. 32
Brundtland Commission 9
Burke, P.F. 22–3, 34
business ethics 1, 9

Cailleba, P. 24, 48
Capaldi, N. 56
Carbon Literacy Training 62
Carrigan, M. 8, 12, 42, 48, 50, 51
Carrington, M.J. 2, 14, 38, 40, 41, 44,
    51, 53, 59, 60
Carroll, A.B. 9–10
Caruana, R. 8, 37–8, 41
Castaldo, S. 11
Casteran, H. 24, 48
Cause-Related Marketing (CRM)
    18–19
Chandler, J.D. 36
Chang, J.C.-J. 18
Chatzidakis, A. 14, 29, 40, 42, 53,
    54
Chen, Y. 19, 55
Cherrier, H. 37, 38, 39, 41, 42, 60
Chowdhury, R.M.M.I. **17**, 19, 27
Clarke, I. 51
Claudy, M.C. 52

clothing 1, 11, 13, 44, 50, 55; ambivalence 31, 34, 52; consumer attitudes 12, 23, 24, 25, 48, 49
Clouder, S. 52
codes of conduct **5**
Colmekcioglu, N. **17**, 19
Connolly, J. 5, 6, 8, 23, 44, 49, 55, 60
consumer activism 1, 4, 6
consumer altruism 26–7
consumer ethics 4, 6, 18, 54, 55
consumer identity projects 38–42
Cooper, T. 49
Cooperative Ethical Consumer Markets report (2021) 11, 12
Cornwell, B. **17**
corporate social responsibility (CSR) 7–8, 9–11, 16, 24, 56
Corsini, F. 38, 42, 45, 46
Cova, B. 15
Cova, V. 15
Covid-19 pandemic 12
Cowe, R. 21, 22
Crane, A. 37
Creyer, E.H. 23
culture 19–20
Cunningham W.H. 16

Dauvergne, P. 4
Davenport, E. **5**, 13
Davies, I.A. 1–2, 12, 24, 25, 44, 61
Dawkins, J. 24
de Groot, J.I.M 4, 26–7, 29, 34, 56, 57
Dekker, D. 32
Deng, X. 11
Department for Environment, Food and Rural Affairs (DEFRA) 22
De Pelsmacker 8, 12, **17**, 18, 20, 34, 57
de Spiegeleer, J. 8
Devinney, T.M. 14, 20–1, 34, 38, 47–8, 49, 51, 56–7, 58, 60–1
Dianati, S. 10, 61
Dickson, M.A. **5**, 28, 38, 48, 51
Djafarova, E. 18, 26, 27

Earle, A.G. 61
Eckhardt, G.M. 14
economic downturns 12
Economist, The 14
'eco' ranges 1–2, 23

Edelman Trust Barometer 10
education 61–2
Elkington, J. 8, 9
emotional outcomes 54–5
Ethical Consumer (magazine) 5
ethical consumption: consumer attitudes towards 23–5; definition 4–6; history 1; increased research 2; at the individual level 12–13; interconnectivity between concerns 6; at the organisational level 10–11; practices 6–7; problems 13–15, 47–58; psychological perspectives 26–36; at the sector level 11–12; segmentation perspectives 16–23; sociological perspectives 37–46
ethical motivation 16, 17, 20, 21–3, 34
ethical obligation 26, 28, 35, 49, 60
ethical pluralism 60
Ethical Trading Initiative (ETI) 13
expectancy-value models 26, 27–9, 56

Fair Trade 1–2, 5, 6, 11, 31, 60; as a mainstream consumer concern 12, 13; problems 8, 14, 57; segmentation perspectives 16, 18, 20, 21, 23, 24
FairTrade Foundation 1
Firat, A.F. 32–3, 39
Fishbein, M. 26, 27
Fisher, J. 9
Fisher, T. 49, 50
Foots, S. 18, 26, 27
Francis, T. 18
Freestone, O.M. 20, 35, 57
fully screened 6

Gabriel, Y. 1
Gallarza, M.G. 35
Garcia-Ruiz, P. 27, 30, 40–1, 42, 43, 45
Gegez, A.E. **17**
gender 18–19
Generation Y 24
Generation Z 18
Giddens, A. 39–40, 41
Giesler, M. 39
Glac, K. 34, 57
Godwin, M.P. 4
Goulding, C. 42

Govind, R. 51, 52
green consumerism 5–6, 28, 49–50, 51, 60
greenwashing 4, 11, 48
Gregory-Smith, D. 54, 55
Griffiths, P. 14
guilt 14, 30, 35, 40, 48, 54–5
Gummerus, J. 35–6, 52
Gutman, J. 30, 31
Gutsche 1–2, 12

habitus 43–4, 45
Ha-Brookshire, J.E. 8, 11, **17**, 18, 24, 34, 56
Halkier, B. 38
Han, T-I. 4, 27
Handelman, J. **17**
Hargreaves, T. 42, 43, 44, 45
Harrison, R. 6, 23, 52
Hassan, L. 14, 35, 49, 50, 51, 52, 54, 57
Hassan, S.M. 17
Hawkins, R. **17**, 18–19, 20
Heath, J. 14
Heinonen, K. 36
Helkkula, A. 36
Heskett, J.L. 35
Hiller, A. 11, 21, 34, 36, 39–40, 55, 56, 61
Hiller Connell, K.Y. 14, 50
Hinman, L.M. 60
Hoefl, F. 18
Hoelscher, V. 42
Hohnen, P. 7
Holbrook, M.B. 35
Hooper, S. 44
Huddart Kennedy, E. 43
Hughes, A. 13
human rights 5, 9, 48
Hustvedt, G. **5**, 28, 38
Hyllegard, K. **5**, 24, 25

Inglehart, R. 13, 41
Iwanow, H. **5**, 25, 48

Jackson, T. 37
Jägel, T. 29, 30–1, 34, 57, 61
Janssen, C. 37
Jayawardhena, C. 11, **17**, 18
Joergens, C. 34, 44, 52, 53

Johnstone, M-L. 14, 35, 44, 51, 52, 53, 57

Kahle, L.R. 32
Kennedy, P. 32
Kim, G.S. **5**, **17**, 20
Kim, S. 23
Kincaid, D.H. 55
knowledge 14, 48–51
Knowles, J. 10
Kozinets, R.V. **17**
Kumar, M. 34, 36, 57
Kuokkanen, H. 11

Lang, T. 1
Lee, K-H. 44
Leyva-de la Hiz, D.I. 61
licensing 53–4
Lim, W.M. **5**, 34, 57
Lister, J. 4
Littler, J. **5**, 14, 48, 57
Littrell, M.A. **5**, 8, 24, 25
Longo, C. 44, 45
Low, W. **5**, 13
Lu, L-C. 26, 60
Luchs, M.G. 34, 36, 57
Luedicke, M.K. **17**, 20, 38, 39, 41
Lundblad, L. 44, 61
Luo, X. 56
Lusch, R.F. 31, 35, 36

Ma, Y.J. **5**, 24, 25, 60
Mahoney, J. 1
Maklan, S. 54–5
Malone, S. 11
Manchiraju, S. 27, 29
Mazar, N. 53–4
McDonald, S. 21
McEachern, M. 24, 35, 57
McGoldrick, P.J. 20, 35, 57
McKinsey 18
McShane, T.O. 35, 57
Memery, J. 5, 11
'middle ground' perspectives 61
Millar, J. 61
Miller, A. 10
Miller, D. 7, 15
Mintel 12
Mish, J. 10
Mohr, L.A. 24

Moisander, J. 35, 57
Monbiot, G. 54
Moor, L. **5**
Moores, T.T. 18
Moosmayer, D. 19, 55
Moraes, C. 8, 11, 13, 14, 37, 42–3, 44, 45, 52
moral norm models 26–7, 29–34, 56
Muncy, J. 4
Murray, J. 39, 41

nationality 20
net-zero 12
neutralisation 53–4
Neville, S. 14
Newholm, T. 1, 2, 6, 14, 37, 48, 51
Ng, I.C.L. 35
Nicholls, A. 21–2
Norum, P.S. 8, 11, **17**, 18, 24, 34, 56

Organisation for Economic Co-operation and Development (OECD) 7–8
Onwezen, M.C. 28, 38, 39, 41
Opal, C. 21–2
organic products 1–2, 5, 6, 11, 28; problems 8, 14; segmentation perspectives 16, 18, 23, 24

Painter, M. 61
Painter-Morland, M. 13, 61, 62
Paolillo, J. **17**, 20
Papaoikonomou, E. 42
paralysis 49–50
Paul, M. 30
Pecoraro, M. 40
Pekerti, A. **17**, 19–20
Peloza, J. **17**, 19
Perera, C. 42, 43, 44, 56, 57
Petro, G. 18
Phipps, M. 37
Pinna, M **17**, 19, 26
Pinto, D.C. 4, **17**, 19
Pivato, S. 11
politics 1, 5, 6, 13, 14, 24, 25
positive purchasing 6, 8, 10, 16, 23, 54
post-purchase evaluations 53, 54, 55–6
Potter, A. 14

Potts, J. 7
practice theory 42–5, 56
Price, M. 61
Prothero, A. 44, 49, 60
psychology 26–36

Ramasamy, B. **17**
Rawwas, M. 18
Reinders, M.J. 41, 42
relationship purchasing 6
religiosity 19–20
Riach, K. 6, 8, 39, 40, 41, 43, 45, 57, 61
Roberts, J.A. 17–18, 20
Robichaud, Z. 18
Rodriguez-Lluesma, C. 27, 30, 40–1, 42, 43, 45
Rokeach, M. 27, 29, 30, 31–2
Røpke, I. 44, 45, 57
Rorty, R. 61
Ross, W.T. 23

Sadachar, A. 27, 29
Sanchez-Fernandez, R. 35
Schaefer, A. 37
Schlegelmilch, B. 21, 24
Schmitt, B. 7
Schmuck, D. 11
Schröder, M.J.A. 24, 35, 57
Schwartz, D.T. 13, 14–15, 52
Schwartz, M.S. 9–10
Schwartz, S.H. 27, 29, 30, 31, 32, **33**, 34
Sebastiani, R. 11
segmentation 16–23
self-identity 26, 28, 38, 43, 49, 53, 60
Shang, J. **17**, 19
Shankar, A. 42
Shaw, D. 5, 6, 8, 23, 27, 28–9, 32, 35, 37, 38, 39, 40, 41, 43, 45, 48, 49, 50, 51, 55, 57, 61
Shepherd, R. 28, 38
Sheppard, B.H. 29
Shiu, E.M.K. 49
Shove, E. 43
Singhapakdi, A. 18
Skålén, P. 42
Smith, L.A. 35
Smith, N.C. 29
Sparks, P. 28, 38

Sreen, N. 26
Steg, L. 29
Stern, P.C. 27, 29
stigma 53
Stobierski, T. 7, 8
Stoel, L. 4, 27
Straughan, R.D. 17–18, 20
Strong, C. 24
Sun, W. 11, 27, 28, 29
supply chains 2, 5, 12–13, 14, 52
sustainability 4, 5, 6, 8–9, 10, 54;
    awareness 49; education 61–2;
    importance to consumers 12, 13;
    segmentation perspectives 22, 24;
    self-identity 41
sweatshops **5**, 48
Szmigin, I. 4, 42

Tadajewski, M. 49–50, 51
Tan, L.P. 14, 35, 51, 52, 53, 57
Tarrant, S.P. 61
Theory of Planned Behaviour (TPB)
    26, 27, 29, 38
Theory of Reasoned Action (TRA)
    26, 27–9
Thiele, L.P. 61
Thøgersen, J. 26, 29, 56
Thompson, C.J. 38, 41, 42, 56
trade-offs 14, 31, 34–5, 36, 37, 45, 48,
    52, 56–8, 61
travel 11, 19, 54
'triple bottom line' 8, 9, 10
Tynan, C. 36

Udell, A.M. 38
uncertainty 14, 49

United Nations Sustainability
    Development Goals 4

Valor, C. **5**, 34, 35, 48, 49, 50, 52, 57
value-belief models 26–7, 29–34,
    56
values 20, 56, 60–1; problems with
    32–4; role of 29–32
Vanhamme, J. 37
Vargo, S.L. 31, 35, 36
Venkatesh, A. 32–3, 39
Veresiu, E. 39
Vitell, S.J. 4, **17**, 20
voluntary simplicity 5, 6, 60

Wagner-Tsukamoto, S 49–50, 51
Warde, A. 38, 42, 43, 44, 45
Webb, D.J. 24
Welzel, C. 13, 41
White, K. 60
Wiggins, D. 60
Williams, S. 21, 22
Wilson, A. 61
Woodall, T. 11, 21, 34, 36, 39–40, 55,
    56, 61
Worcester, R. 24
workers' rights 5

Xu, Y. 11

Yu, H. 18

Zeithaml, V.A. 30, 35
Zeno Group 10
Zhong, C-B. 53–4
Zollo, L. 37

Printed in the United States
by Baker & Taylor Publisher Services